ANTI-SOCIAL BEHAVIOUR AND HOUSING: THE LAW

SIMON COLLINS
and
DEREK O'CARROLL

Distributed jointly by Legal Services Agency Ltd., Fleming House, 134 Renfrew Street, Glasgow G3 6ST and Chartered Institute of Housing in Scotland, 6 Palmerston Place, Edinburgh EH12 5AA.

i

First published by Chartered Institute of Housing in Scotland; Legal Services Agency Ltd; Govan Law Centre; Scottish Legal Education Trust in 1997.

Printed and bound by
Culross the printers
Queen Street
Coupar Angus
Perthshire PH13 9DF

CONTENTS

PREFACE

This book explains the law of Scotland regarding anti-social behaviour in the context of housing. Its main focus is on landlord and tenant law although much of the material, for example the law of interdict and lawburrows, will be of relevance to owner-occupiers. The book also examines alternatives to legal remedies and possible reforms to the law. Although the text is concerned with the law of Scotland, it may also be of interest in England.

The book is intended for use by two groups of practitioners. First, lawyers and others advising on housing law. The second group is housing professionals employed by local authorities, housing associations, Scottish Homes and other landlords. The authors have tried to ensure that the text is as accessible as possible. To this end, legalisms have been avoided where possible or are explained in the text so that the non-lawyer user may still benefit. There is also a glossary and an extensive further reading list in the appendix.

The authors wish to acknowledge the considerable assistance they have received from friends and colleagues in the preparation of this text. Thanks are due to Paul Brown for his help and inspiration in the initial conception of this project, for his comments on the text and his encouragement throughout. We also wish to thank Alan Ferguson and Mike Dailly for their enthusiastic encouragement and practical assistance in the production of this book: We are also indebted to Suzie Scott, Tom Mullen, Paul Brown, Mike Dailly, Robyn McIlroy, Jonathan Mitchell QC, Marion Reid, Jim Bauld, Nicola Wood and Maurice O'Carroll (Snr). They read part or all of the text in draft form and made a number of useful comments and criticisms. We are also indebted to them for providing useful material such as unreported cases and to Suzie Scott in particular for housing research which we would not otherwise have had access to. We would also like to thank Cindy Beck and Iona Stewart for providing supplementary word-processing assistance, to Mary-Jane Bennett for copy-editing and Heather Palomino for proof-reading and both for preparation of tables. The authors, of course, accept full responsibility for any errors and omissions. The law is stated as at 1 January 1996, although it has been possible to incorporate some developments occurring after that date.

Derek O'Carroll
Simon Collins
February 1996

Table of Cases

Table of Cases

A Note on the Cases:

There is a shortage of reported Scottish cases on neighbour nuisance and eviction. We have included as many unreported judgments as possible, mostly from the sheriff court. In some of these, no written judgment was given. These cases, and those of the lower courts in England, should be seen as providing illustration rather than authoritative statements of the law in Scotland. Judgments of the sheriffs principal will provide binding authority on sheriffs within the relevant sheriffdom, and persuasive authority elsewhere. Judgments of the higher English courts, particularly the Court of Appeal, may also be persuasive in Scotland.

Table of Statutes

Table of Statutes

Table of Statutory Instruments

Abbreviations

Case Reports

AC	Appeal Cases
All ER	All England Report
Ch(D)	Chancery (Division)
CLY	Current Law Yearbook
Cr App R	Criminal Appeal Reports
Crim LR	Criminal Law Reports
D	Dunlop (Session Cases)
EG	Estates Gazette
EGCS	Estates Gazette Case Summaries
EGD	Estates Gazette Digest
Env LR	Environmental Law Reports
F	Fraser (Session Cases)
GWD	Greens Weekly Digest
HLR	Housing Law Reports
JC	Justiciary Cases
JLS	Journal of the Law Society of Scotland
JPL	Journal of Planning Law
JP	Justice of the Peace Reports
KB	Kings Bench
LAG	Legal Action Group Bulletin
L Jo	Law Journal
Lloyd's Rep	Lloyd's Reports
LR	Law Reports
M	Macpherson (Session Cases)
Mor	Morrisons Dictionary
NLJ	New Law Journal
NZLR	New Zealand Law Reports
QB	Queen's Bench
R	Rettie (Session Cases)
RVR	Rating and Valuation Reporter
S	Shaw (Session Cases)
SCCR	Scottish Criminal Case Reports
SC	Session Cases; includes Justiciary Cases (JC) and Scottish cases decided in the House of Lords (SC(HL))
SCLR	Scottish Civil Law Reports
SCOLAG	Scottish Legal Action Group Bulletin

Sh Ct Reps	Sheriff Court Reports
SLT	Scots Law Times; includes Sheriff Court Reports (SLT (Sh Ct)), Notes of Recent Decisions (SLT (N)) and decisions of the Lands Tribunal (SLT (Lands Tr))
Sol Jo	Solicitors Journal
TLR	Times Law Reports
(unrep)	Unreported (in standard law reports)
WLR	Weekly Law Reports

Other Abbreviations

BS	British Standard
Cmnd	Command; (Government Report)
et seq	and subsequent pages/paragraphs
HL	House of Lords
IH	Inner House
n	footnote
OCR	Ordinary Cause Rules
OH	Outer House
SCR	Summary Cause Rules
SHLN	Scottish Housing Law News
SI	Statutory Instrument
SLC	Scottish Law Commission

1 INTRODUCTION

Anti-social behaviour by tenants and other occupiers is seen as a large and increasing social problem. Definitions of the problem vary, however, and current responses to it by landlords are inadequate. Further knowledge of its real causes is required.

1.1 'Anti-social Tenants': Defining the Problem

1.1.1 Anti-social behaviour in housing is perceived to be a growing social problem. Such behaviour ranges from the bizarre [1], to the innocuous [2] to the notorious and criminal [3]. Much anger and resentment is caused to suffering neighbours [4]. Defining the problem is controversial in itself, however. The picture presented in the media is one of harassment, violence, and intolerance by malevolent council tenants towards their neighbours: inherently 'bad' people causing deliberate mayhem against a background of social deprivation, drug abuse and criminality. Such representations are simplistic, patronising and inaccurate. They can also lead to misguided attempts at 'solutions'. Hence the present calls for speedier evictions and reduction of security of tenure for council tenants ('getting tough with problem tenants'). This ignores the fact that by no means all neighbour nuisance is caused by tenants. Inevitably, however, even serious commentators differ widely in their approaches to defining and categorising the problem.

[1] See, for example, an unreported case from Kilmarnock Sheriff Court, 16th June 1995, quoted at 1995 SCLR 1018 where a tenant, without permission, kept 'a Vietnamese pot-bellied pig, now deceased ... within the house and garden (together with two Rottweilers'.

[2] *Ball v Ray* 1873 8 Ch 467 – playing of a piano and children's noise (see paragraph 4.5.3 below).

[3] For example *Glenrothes Development Corporation v Graham* (unrep) 14th December 1994, Kirkcaldy Sheriff Court, Sheriff Patrick; discussed at paragraph 10.2.3.10 below together with a list of the behaviour held to have occurred.

[4] Sometimes to an irrational degree. *Unterschutz v Clark* 1994 SCLR 588, for example, gives the full flavour of a neighbour dispute out of control, the sheriff noting that '...[Mrs Unterschutz] wishes to stamp out the practice of having bonfires to burn garden rubbish, at least when the person who lights the bonfire is Mr Clark ... [and so] she and her husband took a hose ... and extinguished a bonfire in Mr Clark's garden. On one such occasion, according to Mr Clark's wife, Mr Unterschutz had asked Mr Clark to go over to where he was. When Mr Clark asked why, Mr Unterschutz said, "So that I can kick your head in". Whether that took place or not is not at issue in this case ...' After an escalation of hostilities, resulting in hospitalisation and arrest, the sheriff noted, "This is not a tale of everyday life in Perth."

1.1.2 Inverness District Council defines anti-social behaviour as 'persistent behaviour by an individual which destroys the quality of life for his/her neighbours'. All other behaviour is simply tenant disputes [1]. Shelter and Scottish Council for Single Homeless define the term as 'behaviour by one household or individual ... which threatens the physical or mental health, safety or security of other households or individuals in the vicinity' [2]. The Scottish Office, in recent guidance, does not define the term but simply gives examples which include criminal behaviour [3]. By contrast, Glasgow District Council attempts to sharply distinguish neighbour disputes (for example, over stair cleaning or 'clash of lifestyles'), anti-social behaviour (for example, behaviour which produces complaints from most tenants in the vicinity or which is a 'serious breach of tenancy conditions') and criminal behaviour [4]. Edinburgh District Council also apparently adopts a tripartite distinction being 'extreme behaviour' (for example, drug dealing, violence), 'serious anti-social behaviour' (for example, threatened violence, vandalism) and other nuisance cases (for example, family disputes, pets, stair cleaning) [5]. Kirkcaldy District Council's anti-social tenants policy conflates those with a history of drug dealing, racial harassment and assault with those who have had rent arrears [6]. The Chartered Institute of Housing in Scotland defines anti-social behaviour as 'actions which include behaviour which may either be criminal such as drug dealing, unprovoked assault [and] racial harassment ...', reserving the term 'nuisance' for 'less serious ... behaviour such as ... pets, stair cleaning, garden upkeep [and] verbal harassment' [7]. Other commentators avoid defining the term entirely or refer to 'neighbour disputes' or 'neighbour nuisance' [8].

[1] Evidence to Scottish Affairs Select Committee on Housing and Anti-Social Behaviour, November 1995.

[2] Ibid.

[3] Scottish Office Environment Department (1995) – such as vandalism, noise, threats of violence, vandalism, joy riding, domestic violence, drugs and other criminal activities.

[4] Evidence to Scottish Affairs Select Committee, November 1995 – such distinctions cannot be mutually exclusive however; take for, example, the use of drugs by a single youth in an established area.

[5] Chartered Institute of Housing in Scotland (1995) *Housing and Anti-social behaviour – Practice Note on the use of legal remedies*, Edinburgh, Scott.S.

[6] *Inside Housing*, 16th September 1994.

[7] Evidence to Scottish Affairs Committee, November 1995. Presumably verbal harassment relating to a neighbours race would be treated differently from verbal harassment relating to, say, a neighbour's personality.

[8] Belgrave (1995) *Nuisance and Harassment: Law and Practice in the Management of Social Housing*, page 3, where all three terms are used but where only nuisance is defined based on the English law of nuisance.

1.1.3 A dictionary provides two quite different definitions of anti-social. First 'avoiding the company of others; unsociable' [1]. Secondly 'contrary or injurious to the interests of society in general' [2]. Clearly, behaviour falling within the first definition could not properly be grounds for complaint, sad though it might be.   Behaviour falling within the second definition could easily be cause for complaint, though surely not only such behaviour. Apart from the dictionary definition [3], 'nuisance' has a quite distinct and different sense in both English and Scots law [4]. The concepts are relative however: one person's anti-social behaviour might   be   another   person's   nuisance,   or   may   be   completely unproblematic to another [5]. Furthermore, causing nuisance or annoyance is itself a ground for eviction [6]. Thus, at least in eviction law, nuisance has rather more serious connotations than apparently intended by those who seek to distinguish nuisance from anti-social behaviour. In the authors' view, the lack of any common definition of what is meant by any of the commonly used terms is inherently intractable.   Too much of the problem is subjective; too much is dependent   on   individual   and   organisational   preconceptions   and localised conditions. It is neither helpful nor necessary to define such terms. A different approach is required.

[1] *Collins Dictionary and Thesaurus* (1987).   The correlates being 'alienated, asocial, misanthropic, reserved, unfriendly, unsociable, withdrawn'.

[2] The correlates being 'antagonistic, belligerent, disorderly, disruptive, hostile, menacing, rebellious'.

[3] 'A person or thing that causes annoyance or bother': *Collins Dictionary and Thesaurus* (1987). The correlates being 'inconvenience, infliction, irritation, offence, pest, problem, trouble, vexation'.

[4] English law categorises nuisance into private, public and statutory. See Belgrave (1995), Chapter 2. For Scots law definitions, see paragraphs 4.5 et seq.

[5] For example, see Clapham et al. (1995) *A Baseline Study of Housing Management in Scotland*: '[Tenants in "better" areas] complain about things that wouldn't be a problem in other areas'; and Aldbourne Associates (1993) *Managing Neighbour Complaints in Social Housing: A Handbook for Practitioners*, paragraph 1.2.1.

[6] Housing (Scotland) Act 1987, Schedule 3, ground 7.

1.1.4 The focus must shift away from trying to determine what constitutes 'anti-social behaviour' or who is a 'problem tenant' and towards dealing with the consequences. In other words, the real issue for landlords is not people's behaviour *per se* but complaints which are made about that behaviour [1]. The object of the housing provider is swift and effective resolution of complaints made to it about tenants' behaviour. Such complaints are to be distinguished from complaints made to the landlord about its own behaviour and require a different type of response [2]. Both Aldbourne Associates and the Institute of Housing strongly recommend, therefore, that landlords apply a coherent approach to complaints about 'neighbour disputes' [3]. Such an approach categorises complaints into three categories. First 'complaints which concern clear breaches of the tenancy conditions and which require a response only from housing management' (such as gardens, cleaning of communal areas). Secondly, 'complaints which require a response from housing management but in conjunction with other agencies' (such as harassment, drug/alcohol abuse with involvement by police, social work or voluntary agencies). Thirdly, complaints which are not housing matters but require referral to other agencies, such as noise (environmental health), harassment of non-tenants (police), clashes of lifestyles (mediation service) [4]. Such an approach has the merit of avoiding the difficulty of categorising behaviour as anti-social or not and emphasises the role of the landlord as manager: its claim being to provide as high quality an environment to all its tenants as possible. Whether the complaint is of late night television or racial harassment, the complainer's life is being disrupted and the landlord has a duty to take whatever steps are in its power and are appropriate to resolve the problem. This must particularly be the case where the behaviour complained of is a breach of the landlord's own tenancy agreement. Two criticisms can, however, be made of this approach. First, it may simply replace the problem of defining terms such as 'anti-social behaviour' with the problem of deciding whether a complaint properly falls into category one, two or three. Secondly, there is a danger, especially in relation to complaints falling within category three, that the landlord may seek to devolve its responsibility for action on to a third party whose actions may be quite ineffective. Where, for instance, a tenant's objectionable behaviour continues even after criminal prosecution, is the landlord simply to wash its hands of the problem leaving the criminal justice system (and the complainant) to its own devices?

[1] Aldbourne Associates (1993), paragraph 1.2.4.

[2] Complaints such as repairs issues or behaviour of housing officers.

[3] Karn et al. (1993) *Neighbour Disputes: Responses by Social Landlords*, Chapter 4; Institute of Housing (1995).

[4] Aldbourne Associates (1993), paragraph 2.2.2.

1.1.5 Throughout this book, the term used is 'anti-social behaviour' or 'anti social conduct'. By this the authors mean any form of behaviour by an occupier which has led or could lead to a complaint by that person's neighbour. In adopting this wide definition, the authors have had regard not only to the other definitions noted above but also to the need to employ a term capable of being used in a text with relative ease, however imperfect. In the authors' view, the appropriate response is to look at the problem created by the people and not to view the people as the problem. The task is to manage behaviour and complaints, not to penalise or stigmatise certain tenants. While the scope of this book is concerned mainly with responses to anti-social behaviour by tenants in the public sector, the problem is in no sense confined to such a group. Tenants of other landlords and owner-occupiers are also reportedly responsible for such conduct [1] or responsible for an increase in complaints [2].

[1] Chartered Institute of Housing in Scotland, Evidence to Scottish Affairs Select Committee November 1995; Aldbourne (1993), paragraph 2.2.2(11). Those concerned with such situations will find Chapters 3 to 6 and 13 of use.

[2] Clapham et al. (1995), paragraph 11.35.

1.1.6 There is a widespread view that anti-social behaviour in tenancies is an increasing problem [1]. There is some evidence to support this. In 1948 only 23% claimed disturbance by external noise at home; this had risen by 50% by 1961 [2]. In 1985/86, 1,270 per million of the population reported domestic noise nuisance to environmental health officers [3]. This had risen to 2,264 per million by 1990/91 [4]. It is certainly not a new problem [5]. Evidence relating to the scale of the problem is patchy. It is suggested that typically 20% of housing officers' time is taken up with dealing with such problems [6]. It is estimated, however, that only 5% of the annual 20,000 actions for recovery of possession concern anti-social behaviour; an average of 17.8 cases per Scottish local authority [7]. There are 731,000 local authority dwellings in Scotland [8]. In the year to October 1995, Glasgow District Council, the largest local authority provider of rented housing, raised 56 court actions against tenants for anti-social behaviour [9]. Inverness District Council estimate that 5% of its tenants 'fall into the anti-social category'[10]. One fifth of tenants interviewed in an authoritative survey said they had had problems with a neighbour [11]. However, most such problems were felt, at least by housing officers, not to be 'serious' [12]. Enquiries to Shelter's Housing Aid Network about neighbour disputes form a tiny proportion of the caseload [13]. Clackmannan District Council have found a very low proportion of such cases [14] in contrast to Edinburgh District Council [15] and Aberdeen District Council [16]. Research in the early 1980's suggested that the problem was quite small in Glasgow [17].

[1] See, for example, Chartered Institute of Housing evidence to Scottish Affairs Select Committee, November 1995; Karn et al. (1993), paragraph 1.1. Clapham (1995), paragraph 11.34.

[2] Wilson Committee on the Problem of Noise (1963) *Noise: Final Report*, Cmnd 2056. Noise is undoubtedly the major source of all complaints about anti-social neighbour behaviour. In descending order of frequency, complaints have been found to relate to amplified music, pets (together accounting for two-thirds of all noise complaints), DIY, voices (particularly children), and car repairs. There is increasing evidence on the adverse effects of noise on health, including mental health, and it has been estimated that in recent years as many as 20 people may have died as a result of domestic noise nuisance, including death from heart attacks, suicide, and murder: see Penn: (1995) *'Noise Control: the law and its enforcement'*(Shaw & Sons).

[3] Hughes (1992) Environmental Laws, Chapter 2.

[4] IEHO (1992) *Environmental Health Statistics 1990/91*. In England and Wales complaints to environmental health officers about noise increased from 31,000 in 1980 to 111,515 in 1992/93 (DoE et al. (1995)).

[5] Submission by Shelter to Scottish Affairs Select Committee, November 1995.

[6] Aldbourne Associates (1993), paragraph 1.2.2. However, only 8 out of the 47 landlords surveyed monitored the number of cases or amount of staff time.

[7] Shelter submission to Scottish Office on Probationary Tenancies (1995).

[8] Scottish Office Statistical Bulletin, HSG/1995/4, May 1995.

[9] Evidence to Scottish Affairs Select Committee, November 1995.

[10] Ibid.

[11] Clapham et al. (1995), paragraph 11.85.

[12] Ibid., paragraph 11.36

[13] Around 2%; submission to Scottish Affairs Select Committee, November 1995.

[14] 56 cases from 1985 to 1988 out of a housing stock of 8,700; ibid.

[15] 300 neighbour complaints per month; ibid.

[16] 15 to 20 complaints a day about anti-social behaviour and 13 to 14 severe cases a month, *Glasgow Herald*, 10th November 1995.

[17] 688 complaints out of a housing stock of 170,000, Eldridge et al. (1982) *Neighbour Disputes: The Response of Glasgow's Housing Department to Tenants' Complaints.*

1.2 Causes of anti-social tenant behaviour

Numerous factors have been adduced to explain why complaints about anti-social behaviour appear to be increasing. Landlords suggest the phenomenon may be due to

- change in standards and expectations leading to friction between the young and old;

- impact of 'right to buy' legislation leading to less tolerance from former council tenants;

- impact of Care in the Community policies, leading to vulnerable and mentally ill people being housed without adequate support;

- changing patterns of housing tenure leading to marginalisation of social rented housing [1];

- increase in statutory rights for tenants and participation in management leading to vocalisation of complaints that might hitherto have been suppressed;

- substantial media coverage of certain notorious cases [2];

- changing work patterns leading to increased occupation of homes and use at unusual hours [3];

- operation of allocations systems and the homelessness legislation;

- increasing ownership of noise-making products in the home: televisions, hi-fis, washing machines, etc;

- poor standards of building design in houses built in the 1950's and 1960's (especially in relation to noise insulation);

- 'remote' housing management [4].

The evidence, such as it is, is largely inconclusive. Nevertheless, the issue of dealing with anti-social behaviour in rented housing is of great concern to housing providers and tenants. For landlords, the issue is not only to do with their responsibility to provide as good a living environment as possible for their tenants. It also has a significant effect on other aspects of housing management such as the level of voids, turnover and rent arrears. For tenants affected by such behaviour, the issue is quality of life – and in extreme cases, life itself [5].

[1] Aldbourne Associates (1993), paragraph 1.2.2, and Shelter submission to Scottish Affairs Committee.

[2] Shelter, ibid. Such as the Grahams of Kirkcaldy and the Fosters of Foyers.

[3] Belgrave (1995), Chapter 1.

[4] Scott, S. (1991) Neighbour Disputes: Is there an Answer?; page 5.

[5] See Scotland on Sunday, 4th September 1994 for a case where a tenant, tormented by his neighbour's television, was convicted of his manslaughter, and received probation. Also, The Herald, 10th November 1995, reporting that suicide and killing have resulted from anti-social behaviour.

1.3 Current Responses

The options open to a landlord are many. In the second chapter we summarise the non-legal, or management options that are available to landlords. The evidence is that insufficient use is being made of such approaches: in particular, mediation is grossly under-utilised. Most cases of anti-social behaviour are amenable to such an approach. However, the authors recognise that legal options may require to be used instead of, following, or in conjunction with a management approach. In general, it appears to us that eviction is overused by social landlords and frequently viewed as the first, main, or best legal weapon to use when dealing with anti-social tenants. No doubt in some cases it becomes unavoidable. As the following chapters show, however, the legal options are more varied than simple eviction. Again, our experience suggests that these remedies are under-utilised, and that the coordinated inter-agency approach required to obtain maximum benefit from their use is often lacking. If resource deficiencies are at the root of this failure (and no doubt they play a significant part), then the price for not making such resources available is being paid not only by victims of anti-social behaviour, but also by those made homeless through eviction.

1.4 About this Book

The object of this book is to detail and explain the legal remedies available to deal with anti-social behaviour by occupiers. We also outline some of the current and competing proposals for reform. Our focus is on public sector tenants, but much of the law discussed will also apply to other tenants and also to owner-occupiers. We do not suggest that the law can provide a solution to anti-social tenant behaviour. Our central concern is to assist occupiers and housing managers to find ways to more effectively use the law to deal with anti-social behaviour and, in particular, to find alternatives to eviction. Wherever possible, eviction should be regarded very much as the 'last resort'. Where eviction is the most appropriate solution, it should be proceeded with as efficiently as possible.

2. ALTERNATIVES TO LEGAL ACTION

This text is primarily concerned with the law. However, there is considerable scope for tackling the problem without invoking legal remedies. Landlords can achieve a significant impact by the use of modern estate management techniques. No one course of action is likely to be sufficient in itself. A successful strategy will be one which is comprehensive and flexible and which involves all the relevant individuals and agencies.

Outlined in this chapter are the features likely to be found in a successful estate management strategy designed to deal effectively with complaints about tenant neighbours. The composite elements may be roughly divided into those which are preventative (or proactive) and those which are responsive (or reactive). Careful preparation, implementation and monitoring of the strategy is required. The reward is likely to be substantially increased tenant and housing staff satisfaction and a decreased reliance on legal remedies [1].

[1] For further information on good practice in managing neighbour complaints see particularly the following: Aldbourne Associates (1993), *Managing Neighbour Complaints in Social Housing: A Handbook for Practitioners*, Aldbourne Associates; Chartered Institute of Housing (1995) *Housing Management Standards Manual*, CIoH; Scott, Suzie (ed.) (1991) *Neighbour disputes: Is there an Answer*, Tenants Participation Advisory Service (Glasgow); Scott, Suzie (ed.) (1994) *Housing and Anti-Social Behaviour; the Way Ahead*, Chartered Institute of Housing in Scotland; University of Stirling in association with the Chartered Institute of Housing in Scotland (1995) *Good Practice in Housing Management: Guidance Note No. 5, Tenancy Management*, Scottish Office; Karn et al. (1993) *Neighbour Disputes: Responses by Social Landlords*, Institute of Housing; Scott, Suzie (1994) *Reviewing Good Practice* (IoHiS Conference Paper), Glasgow University Centre for Housing Research and Urban Studies; National Consumer Council (1991); *Housing Complaints Procedures*, National Consumer Council; Quayle and Wellings, *Principles of Good Practice for Social Landlords*, 'Taking the anti out of anti-social', Inside Housing 15th July 1994 Hull District Council; Department of the Environment (1989) *Tackling Racial Violence and Harassment*, HMSO. See also the extensive reading list contained in the Appendix to this book.

2.1 Preventative Measures

2.1.1 Objectives and Policies

The most comprehensive research carried out in Scotland to date has found that nearly half of the landlords surveyed did not have written policies, procedures or guidance for staff on neighbour nuisance [1]. Scottish Office guidance emphasises the importance of clear objectives and policies and gives examples of these [2]. Other commentators on good practice likewise place importance on the need for clear management objectives and policies as a requirement for effectively tackling neighbourhood nuisance [3]. Selected aspects of effective policies in this area are touched on in the following paragraphs.

[1] Clapham et al. (1995) *A Baseline Study of Housing Management in Scotland* (Scottish Office), paragraphs 11.12 and 11.38. This failure in itself arguably leaves local authority landlords open to charges of maladministration in respect of complaints to the Ombudsman about any failure to deal effectively with anti-social neighbours.

[2] Stirling University (1995), supra, Chapters 3 and 4.

[3] See especially Aldbourne Associates (1993), Chapter 2; and Karn et al., Chapter 4.

2.1.2 Tenancy Agreements

It is important that the tenancy agreement clearly indicates to the incoming tenant his/her responsibilities in relation to neighbour nuisance. The vast majority of tenancy agreements offered by public sector landlords appear to contain some form of prohibition of anti-social behaviour [1]. The comprehensiveness and quality of these clauses may be lacking [2]. While the absence of clear and comprehensive provisions may not prejudice subsequent eviction action [3], legal action for interdict may fail in the absence of a contractual provision prohibiting certain behaviour [4]. In any event, a clear indication in writing to the new tenant of what behaviour is prohibited together with a statement of what will happen if that behaviour occurs is an important part of a preventative strategy [5]. For example, Clackmannan District Council visit the tenant a few weeks after letting to review the council's policies with the tenant and to explain how to proceed in the event of any complaints or concerns. Scottish Homes in Windlaw, Castlemilk, Glasgow has developed a Good Neighbour Agreement which sets out the obligations and expectations of both landlord and tenants. Glasgow District Council has developed the concept of 'Estate Action Plans' which incorporate the idea of using the tenancy agreement to help improve the quality of life on housing schemes. It is signed by the tenant at the same time as the tenancy agreement and has contractual effect [6]. A similar process is carried out by Westminster City Council [7].

[1] Clapham et al. (1995), paragraph 11.8: 69 out of 71 of those surveyed.

[2] Ibid.; for example, only five landlords had clauses specifically prohibiting racial harassment. See Marion Reid (1996), Housing and anti-social behaviour, practice note on the use of legal remedies, Chartered Institute of Housing in Scotland, page 8 for examples of better versions. See also 10.1.3 *et seq*. below.

[3] Because various types of behaviour are specifically covered by the statutory eviction grounds: see paragraph 10.2 below. Note also that the effect of the Unfair Terms in Consumer Contracts Regulations 1995 (SI 1994/3159), which came into effect on 1st July 1995, is that terms of a standard form tenancy agreement entered into after that date may not be enforceable if they are unfair. The Regulations provide that terms in a tenancy agreement must be in plain, intelligible language.

[4] See paragraphs 4.3 and 4.4 below.

[5] See Stirling University, Chapter 5.

[6] Stirling University at paragraph 7.2.1.

[7] Aldbourne Associates (1993), at paragraph 3.2.1.

2.1.3 Staff Issues

Staff of landlords must be properly trained, supported and resourced. The extent of training needs to be linked to the policies and objectives. The staff must understand the policies, be trained in the established procedures and work consistently to them. The trend to generic working patterns places considerable demands on staff and a more general review of tenancy management services and staff qualifications required may be necessary. Training of front-line staff in areas such as the defusing of violence and aggression may be necessary [1]. Staff will need access to specialist resources, such as legal advice. Alternatively, consideration could be given to deploying a specialist case worker to deal with tenants who make large demands on the housing service [2].

[1] Stirling University (1995), paragraph 4.2. Many staff do not feel adequately trained in this area: Clapham et al. (1995).

[2] For example, Cynan Valley District Council. See Aldbourne Associates (1993), paragraph 3.2.2. Renfrew District Council is one authority which employs specialist workers to deal with problems in this area.

2.1.4 Allocation Policies

Complaints about behaviour often arise from lifestyle differences [1]. For example, placing a young family in a flat over a retired couple is likely to produce complaints about noise. Landlords could consider the household composition of adjoining flats as part of a more sensitive allocations policy. Some landlords have used quotas to restrict (or increase) the numbers of young families occupying flats [2]. Separating young people into their own managed accommodation may be considered or creating 'mature' blocks for older households [3].

[1] Clapham et al. (1995), paragraph 11.36; and Scott (1991), page 35.

[2] For example Clackmannan District Council. See Shelter *Submission to the Scottish Affairs Committee on Neighbour Nuisance*, November 1995, page 5.

[3] Clapham et al. (1995), paragraph 11.36. Great care, however, requires to be taken in implementing such strategies to ensure that discrimination against such groups does not occur.

2.1.5 Tenant Participation

Participation by tenants in the management of their own housing is now generally recognised as an essential component of good practice [1]. Tenant participation is said to assist better housing management, provide tenants with more choice, increase customer satisfaction, and aid community development. Methods include provision of written information, surveys, representation on committees and regular liaison between tenants' groups and the landlord. The processes involved will vary according to the issue, the type of landlord and kind of tenant group. The processes can be seen as a spectrum of increasing involvement ranging from passive receivers of information at one end to actual control over the provision of some or all aspects of housing provision at the other [2]. Housing co-operatives who have used tenant participation as an important and effective means of tackling neighbour nuisance include Hawthorne and Calvay, both in Glasgow [3]. Dumbarton and Stirling District Councils both produced and distributed leaflets to their tenants narrating their policies. Dunfermline District Council formulated its policy on anti-social behaviour with tenants' organisations. Clackmannan District Council did so in the context of a multi-agency forum. In Denmark tenants have the right to elect the majority of the housing provider's executive board, which, among other functions, is responsible for setting and monitoring policy. Tenants thus have substantial influence over planning. Tenants have a responsibility for preventing and dealing with problems between neighbours and they set the estate rules which bind all tenants. As a result, tenant satisfaction is high and the eviction rate is low [4].

[1] See, for example, Institute of Housing (1990) *Tenant Participation in Housing Management*, Institute of Housing and Tenants Participation Advisory Service and the references cited therein at Chapter 1. See also University of Stirling/Chartered Institute of Housing in Scotland (1994), Good Practice Note No. 4: Tenant Participation, Scottish Office. Also Scott (1991), pages 21 and 36.

[2] Institute of Housing (1990), Chapter 1.

[3] Scott (1991), page 23.

[4] J.N. Moller (1993); Non-Profit housing in Denmark, Interplan, No. 7, Denmark; Aldbourne Associates (1993), paragraph 3.7.

2.1.6 Housing and Estate Design

Design of houses/flats and estates may cause or contribute to anti-social behaviour and crime [1]. For example noise, the major source of complaints [2], is often related to insufficient sound insulation [3]. Improving standards of noise insulation in a systematic manner, for example during scheduled renovation work, is likely to reduce complaints. Design of estates can be improved to reduce crimes such as vandalism, housebreaking or drug abuse, the first two of which cause not only nuisance to neighbours but result in increased costs to landlords [4]. Design-led initiatives to reduce crime may include measures such as the installation of entry-phones, improved lighting, secure fencing, etc. More radical measures include the installation of closed circuit television cameras and concierge systems in tower blocks [5] and the installation of CCTV systems in the streets of estates such as Gowktrapple, Wishaw [6] and the East End of Newcastle [7]. These latter measures have, however, important civil liberties implications which appear to have been largely neglected in the search for alternative strategies. Other measures could include a reduction in shared access to accommodation and careful siting of amenity areas and children's play areas [8].

[1] Scott (1991), pages 6 and 34.

[2] Clapham et al. (1995), paragraph 11.35.

[3] Department of Environment (1995); *Neighbour Noise Working Party: Review of the Effectiveness of Neighbour Noise Controls*; Dept. of Environment, Welsh Office and Scottish Office; paragraph 7.1. In England and Wales, there were 111,515 complaints of noise nuisance to Environmental Health Departments in 1992/93. The Scottish figure for the same period was 1,950.

[4] Bannister and Kearns (1995), *Managing Crime: findings from a survey of Scottish Housing Initiatives*, Chartered Institute of Housing. See also Chartered Institute of Housing (1995), *Housing and Crime: how well are we managing*, CIoH.

[5] For example, the Red Road and Mitchellhill flats in Glasgow where the district council's initiative has led to a dramatic reduction of crime and neighbour complaints; Scott (1991), page 28.

[6] By Motherwell District Council *The Herald*, 28th December 1994.

[7] *Independent on Sunday*, 3rd September 1995. The powers of local authorities to provide closed circuit television have now been clarified by section 163 of the Criminal Justice and Public Order Act 1994. The cameras must be provided to promote the prevention of crime, and may only be installed after consultation with the chief constable of the area.

[8] Scott (1991), page 34. For further sources on crime and housing see Bannister and Kearns (1995); Scottish Office Environment Dept. (1994a) *Housing and Crime Prevention*, Circular 2/1994, Scottish Office; Scottish Office Environment Dept. (1994) *Planning for Crime Prevention: Planning Advice Note*, HMSO.

2.1.7 Vetting of Tenants

A few local authorities have introduced tenant vetting schemes whereby applicants for housing are investigated and those who, in the opinion of the council, have a history of anti-social behaviour or rent arrears, are refused a tenancy or a transfer of tenancy. Dundee District Council vetted 6,633 applicants for the waiting or transfer list in the 12 months beginning October 1991 (the beginning of the scheme). This resulted in the removal of only 29 applicants (0.4%) at a cost of £268,064 [1]. Kirkcaldy District Council have implemented a similar policy. That council's sanction is suspension from the waiting list for a period of between one and ten years [2]. Both councils have attracted considerable criticism on several grounds. First, many doubt that the equiparation of rent arrears with anti-social behaviour is defensible. Secondly, the local authority may be failing in their legal obligations in relation to admission to waiting lists [3]. Thirdly, there is a danger that in at least some cases, applicants may be wrongly denied access to the relevant list on the basis of inaccurate or misleading information [4]. Fourthly, there is no formal requirement to give full written reasons for refusal. Finally, no formal adequate means of appeal are provided. Whether local authorities, whose duties and responsibilities range far wider than simply those of the landlord, should be involved in restricting access to accommodation which is often housing of last resort is, to say the least, debatable.

[1] Report by Director of Housing to Chief Executive, Dundee District Council, 10th March 1993. The scheme has, however, continued.

[2] *Inside Housing,* 16th September 1994.

[3] See sections 19 and 20, Housing (Scotland) Act 1987. Certain applicants are entitled to a reasonable preference – section 20 (1).

[4] This may give grounds for judicial review – see, for example, *R v Islington London Borough Council ex parte Aldabbagh* (1994) 27 HLR 271, DC.

2.2   Responsive Measures

2.2.1   The majority of tenants who have made complaints to their landlord regarding anti-social behaviour are dissatisfied or very dissatisfied with the response of their landlord [1]. This may well be because few landlords have a cohesive strategy for managing neighbour complaints and tend to deal with complaints on an ad hoc and reactive basis [2]. A comprehensive strategy will include well-developed procedural guidelines for dealing with complaints about anti-social behaviour [3].   According to the National Consumer Council there should be an emphasis on early resolution of complaints, clear and publicised procedures, proper record keeping and a positive conciliatory approach [4]. Guidance from the Local Government Ombudsman suggests alternative principles of accessibility, simplicity, speed, objectivity, confidentiality, consistency and flexibility [5]. Guidance published by the Housing Association Ombudsman, established in 1994, makes it clear that housing association landlords must maintain proper documentation which must be made available to the Ombudsman in the event of a complaint to him/her [6]. The procedures to be adopted may vary from landlord to landlord.   Substantial guidance is available [7].

[1] Clapham et al. (1995), paragraph 11.91. The baseline for the survey was 71 public sector landlords.

[2] Aldbourne Associates (1993), paragraph 1.2.3.

[3] Aldbourne Associates (1993), Chapters 1 and 2; Karn et al. (1993), Chapter 4.

[4] National Consumer Council (1991).

[5] Commissioner for Local Government in Scotland – Annual Report 1993.

[6] See annual report 1995.

[7] For example, Aldbourne Associates (1993), Chapter 2; Chartered Institute of Housing (1995); Scott, Suzie (ed.) (1994); Karn et al. (1993). See also Scottish Homes and SFHA, Good Practice in Housing Management Standards Manual (1993), Scottish Homes, which details recommended practice for housing associations in the management of complaints.

2.2.2 Multi-Agency Approaches

Recent research reports clearly identify the need for landlords to co-operate closely with a variety of different agencies [1]. These may include: local authority departments (for example environmental health, social work, education, legal services, planning), police, voluntary groups (for example mediation, self-help groups, law centres, CABx), other housing providers, health boards. Setting up arrangements for multi-agency working may not be easy. It requires a clear lead and commitment from senior management, joint training sessions to develop understanding of the other agency, regular liaison and updating [2]. In Scotland at least, while informal liaison agreements are common, formal ones are much less so [3]. Formal agreements have been reached by Stirling District Council, Central Region and Clackmannan District Council amongst others [4].

[1] See Stirling University (1995), paragraph 4.3; Clapham et al. (1995), paragraph 11.49

[2] Aldbourne Associates (1993), paragraphs 3.6 *et seq*. These paragraphs also contain useful examples of successful agreements and practices.

[3] Clapham et al. (1995), paragraph 11.50.

[4] In Clackmannan, the 'Anti-Social Behaviour Liaison Group' comprises three council departments, councillors, police, social work, the Citizens' Advice Bureau, the Health Board and housing associations. In Central Region, the 'Partnership in Action' comprises the district councils, the regional council, police and the Race Equality Council. The agreement in both groups is to improve sharing of information and increase effectiveness of joint working.

2.2.3 Mediation and Arbitration

Arbitration seeks to resolve disputes by instituting a process whereby an independent third party, after investigation, offers or imposes a solution. Glasgow District Council has such a scheme [1]. Mediation, by contrast, is a process wherein an independent third party attempts to facilitate a solution mutually acceptable to the disputants. Although mediation is not suitable for all disputes, it is being used increasingly in the UK and its use is encouraged by the Department of Environment [2] and other commentators on good practice [3]. Mediation is a step by step process where the parties reach an agreement through the mediator as to future behaviour or action. It is particularly suitable where the relationship between the disputants is important, where both parties are willing to work towards a solution and legal action is not appropriate. It can assist in disputes involving owner occupiers as well as tenants. It separates the significant from the dramatic, encourages the parties to agree responsibilities rather than ascribe blame, and to look to the future: 'it turns a two-way fight into a three-way search for a solution' [4]. Mediation can be provided as an independent community mediation service, as in-house mediation or by the employment of freelance mediators. However, the use of in-house mediators undermines impartiality which many see as an essential ingredient of mediation. Mediation is used by a number of housing providers in England [5]. In Scotland, by contrast, mediation is little used [6]. Edinburgh District Council and SACRO [7] have established a mediation service focused on peripheral estate housing offices. Dundee District Council also operates a community mediation scheme. SACRO itself operates a Reparation and Mediation Project which links into the criminal justice system. Cases are referred to it by the procurator fiscal. Those referred to it have been charged with criminal offences against someone with whom they have some sort of continuing relationship: neighbour, friend, relative, partner, etc. Before making a decision on whether to prosecute, the accused and the victim are offered mediation. If successful, the procurator fiscal invariably drops the charges. SACRO claim a success rate of 82% [8]. A community mediation project is presently being piloted by Citizens Advice Scotland (the representative body of Citizens Advice Bureaux), which takes referrals from CABx. This initiative is still in the early stages of its development and meaningful success rates are not yet available. Clearly, in Scotland, there is considerable room for improvement in the use of this valuable tool. The costs involved are not large, certainly in comparison with the costs of the alternative. Mediation, especially if used at the early stages of a dispute, has the potential to save local agencies money, time and hassle [9].

[1] The tenants have a contractual right to access to an Arbitration Tribunal (comprising representatives of the Council and tenants and an independent chairperson) in cases involving disputes with the housing department. In 1993, 63 applications were made but all bar 6 were resolved prior to the hearing. At present, the arbitration scheme specifically excludes complaints about anti-social behaviour. Stirling University (1995), paragraph 7.2.2.

[2] See Department of Environment (1994) *Mediation: Benefits and Practice*, Department of Environment. This is an excellent introduction to mediation and contains many useful references. It is claimed that, since 1984, over 10,000 neighbour disputes have been resolved by mediation; 60% of these noise related.

[3] Stirling University (1995), paragraph 7.2.2; Karn et al. (1993), Chapters 5 and 6; Aldbourne Associates (1993), paragraph 3.5.

[4] Department of Environment (1994) *Mediation: Benefits and Practice*, Chapter 2.

[5] See, for examples, cases cited in Aldbourne Associates (1993), paragraphs 3.5 *et seq.*; Dept. of Environment (1994), Chapter 3; Karn et al. (1993); Scott (1991), page 32. Contact Mediation UK, an umbrella organisation of mediation services, for more information: 82A Gloucester Road, Bristol BS7 8BN, telephone 0117 924 1234.

[6] Clapham et al. (1995), paragraph 11.47. Only one respondent housing provider (out of 71) had an in-house mediation team. Only 11 said they would opt for conciliation/mediation which, however, was attempted by front-line housing officers.

[7] Scottish Association for the Care and Rehabilitation of Offenders. There is a similar project in Fife, which commenced in late 1995, also involving SACRO.

[8] Information given to the authors by SACRO. There is also evidence that suggests that such schemes involve a significant cost saving – between £352 and £506 per case: *Neighbourhood Disputes in the Criminal Justice System*: Scottish Office Central Research Unit.

[9] Mediation cases cost on average £200 to £300 per case, though not all mediators charge; Dept. of Environment (1994), Chapter 4.3. See *Scotland on Sunday* (Spectrum), 25th June 1995 for an example, where Inverness District Council evicted a couple with children and did not attempt mediation 'because of the costs.' They then charged that family £473.70 for two weeks' bed and breakfast accommodation. See also Professor David Donnison's essay on the subject (*Scotland on Sunday*, 2nd July 1995).

2.2.4 Intensive Care

Dundee District Council has obtained urban aid funding amounting to £1 million, to deal with tenants who have already been evicted as a result of their anti-social behaviour. The district council is to work with the National Children's Home and Tayside Regional Council in refurbishing a block of council housing to provide four furnished flats for families who have been evicted, plus office accommodation for 14 staff providing 24-hour cover. Another six houses scattered throughout Dundee will be used as the next step for families who have had six months 'intensive care' in the central block. The objective is to provide such families with an opportunity to re integrate themselves into the community [1]. This innovative approach has the merit of addressing the most negative aspect of eviction: that the problem is simply pushed elsewhere rather than directly confronted. However, some have expressed concern at aspects of this project relating principally to the very intensive 'special skills schooling' apparently applied and the restriction of freedom imposed on the families thus housed.

[1] *The Herald*, 8th December 1994.

2.3 An Incremental Approach to Neighbour Nuisance Complaints

The ultimate disposal of a complaint will of course vary according to its type and severity. The authors advocate an incremental strategy with the severity of sanction gradually increasing. In our view, it is only once all alternatives have been tried and failed, or examined and rejected for sound reasons, that permanent eviction should be contemplated. The causes of anti-social behaviour are rarely simple. The solutions are unlikely to be straight-forward. Landlords who adopt a punitive or legalistic response are failing to properly manage their housing stock. A complainer is entitled to a swift and appropriate response from the landlord; one that is likely to produce a change which is acceptable to all. On the other hand, the person or persons complaining may not themselves be in the right. An effective anti-social behaviour policy will be sensitive and flexible to the individual circumstances of the case, making use of the wide range of legal and non legal tools available. If, on the other hand, the only tool the landlord knows how to use is a hammer, every problem begins to look like a nail.

Internal management	- personal visit by housing officer
	- letter(s) from housing officer
	- conciliation
	- housing improvement (for example, sound insulation)
	- final warning
	- management transfer
Inter-agency	- refer for counselling/advice
	- refer for action by other agency, for example:
	- police
	- environmental health
	- social work
	- liaise with other agency for action
Third-party assistance	- mediation
	- arbitration
Legal action	- interdict/lawburrows
	- statutory notice/environmental law remedy
	- eviction - alternative accommodation
	- eviction - no alternative accommodation

3 LOCAL AUTHORITY POWERS AND THE CRIMINAL LAW

Most neighbour nuisance is a criminal offence. This sometimes seems to be forgotten. Criminal law sanctions should be applied to criminal behaviour, not eviction. There is no shortage of laws prohibiting anti-social behaviour by neighbours. The power to investigate and prosecute offences lies with the police and procurator fiscal, although local authorities have other relevant legal powers. A close co-operative approach is likely to be most effective in tackling neighbour nuisance.

3.1 Powers and Duties: Police and Procurator

3.1.1 In Scotland, the duties to investigate and prosecute crime almost always fall onto the police and procurator fiscal respectively [1]. Accordingly (and unlike the position in England and Wales), it is seldom open to social landlords such as local authorities to take the lead role in dealing with neighbour nuisance through the criminal justice system [2]. The police and fiscal service, however, do not have the same degree of direct accountability to 'aggrieved neighbours' as the local authority. It is the local authority as social landlord who bears the brunt of neighbour complaints, not the prosecutor. This, together with the pressure on the criminal justice system to prosecute 'serious' crimes and an apparent lack of resources for even this task [3], may lead to under-utilisation of the available laws to prosecute neighbour nuisance offences, or at least those that fall short of physical violence. Whoever has the lead role in prosecution, resources must be made available to do it effectively.

[1] Detailed textbooks are available on the nature and procedure of the criminal law and criminal justice system: see Sheriff Gordon, *Criminal Law* (Greens, 2nd edition, 1978) & Second Cumulative Supplement (1992); Renton and Brown, *Criminal Procedure* (Greens, 5th edition) (references in this text are to the 14th release: 1st January 1995); Bradley & Shields Criminal Procedure (Scotland) Act 1995 (annotated) Greens, 1995.

[2] Notwithstanding section 189 of the Local Government (Scotland) Act 1973: see *Inverness-shire County Council v Weir* 1938 JC 11; *McKinstry v County Council of Lanark* 1962 JC 16. There are minor statutory exceptions – for example, the Education (Scotland) Act 1980, section 43(2): prosecution of parents for truancy of their children. In practice, however, even these prosecutions are delegated to the procurator fiscal.

[3] One well publicised example from Falkirk Sheriff Court concerned the 'freeing' from prosecution of a number of accused persons due to stand trial for summary offences due to the lack of any available prosecuting lawyers. A handwritten note to this effect was pinned to the door of the court room on the morning the cases were due to be heard.

3.1.2 Once a decision to prosecute has been taken [1], it is for the public prosecutor to conduct the case on behalf of the state as s/he thinks fit. In other words, the matter is taken out of the hands of the original victim or complainer. If the fiscal decides, for example, to accept a guilty plea to a lesser charge than the one originally brought, or at some stage to drop the prosecution, then these are not decisions in which the victim has a say.

[1] On the factors which should inform this decision, see Renton and Brown, paragraph 3.01. They include considering whether the act or omission charged is of sufficient importance to be made the subject of a criminal prosecution, and also whether the information leading to the charging of the accused has been inspired by malice or ill-will.

3.1.3 A wide range of criminal offences are commonly applicable to neighbour disputes. A particular investigating officer may, however, not be aware that certain conduct constitutes an offence. Given the range of statutory offences available, this is hardly surprising. If a constable simply refuses to investigate conduct which, for example, is an offence under the Civic Government (Scotland) Act 1982, section 49(4) or under the Environmental Protection Act 1990, section 87, then this may be the subject of a complaint to the Chief Constable for the area [1]. The fact that interdict or eviction may also be available remedies does not remove the obligation on the police to investigate crime [2]. Clearly, however, a co-operative approach between police and local authority is preferable [3].

[1] See Police (Discipline) (Scotland) Regulations 1967, SI 1967/1021 (as amended by SI 1972/777, SI 1975/1544, SI 1976/1073, SI 1982/902 and SI 1987/2226), Schedule 1; see in particular 'wilful or careless neglect of duty'. On powers and duties of police generally see *Stair Memorial Encyclopaedia*, Vol. 16 (1995), paragraphs 1701-1822.

[2] Police (Scotland) Act 1967, section 17(1). Similarly with conduct which is in breach of an existing interdict. Although breaching an interdict is not in itself a criminal offence, if it involves conduct which is, then the fact that there exists the right to bring civil proceedings for the breach does not absolve the police from arresting, detaining or charging the perpetrator, as need be (note: only interdicts by one spouse against another may have a statutory 'power of arrest' attached by the court – Matrimonial Homes (Family Protection) (Scotland) Act 1981, section 15).

The (English) Housing Act 1996 allows for the attachment of a power of arrest to injunctions (interdicts) taken by local authorities and other social landlords against breaches of leases by anti-social tenants. Such powers do not apply to Scotland.

[3] For example, the joint Scottish Office/Department of Environment Working Party on Neighbour Noise (Department of Environment 1995) recommends that a code of good practice be issued jointly by professional representative bodies to police forces and local authorities to encourage effective local arrangements for dealing with noise complaints.

3.1.4 It is evidentially more difficult to obtain a conviction for a criminal offence than to obtain decree in a civil action – for example an eviction. Unlike in civil cases, there must normally be corroboration of any criminal charge [1] unless there is statutory provision to the contrary [2]. In practical terms this often means other neighbours providing witness statements for the police and giving evidence in court, which they may be reluctant to do [3]. There is nothing to prevent a housing authority's 'professional witnesses' being used to provide evidence to corroborate charges brought in the criminal courts. In addition, of course, any criminal charge must be proved beyond reasonable doubt rather than on a civil 'balance of probabilities' [4].

[1] *Morton v HMA* 1938 JC 50 at 55; Renton and Brown, paragraph 18.52; and see paragraph 13.5.2 below.

[2] For example, a contravention of section 87 of the Environmental Protection Act 1990: see paragraph 3.3.11 below.

[3] The prosecutor can compel any competent witness, properly cited, to attend court. Failure to comply with a citation is likely to be deemed to be contempt of court, and is punishable by fine or imprisonment: Renton and Brown, paragraph 18.104. On a practical level of course, the procurator may be unwilling to force a witness to attend where it is clear that he or she is likely to be hostile in giving evidence.

[4] See *McKenzie v HMA* 1959 JC 32 at 36–7 and Renton and Brown, paragraph 18.02. See also paragraph 13.3 below.

3.2 Powers and Duties: Local Authorities

Local authorities possess a range of powers to regulate and enforce matters relevant to neighbour nuisance. These may or may not have relevance in any particular case. Intervention by means of these powers, where appropriate, should at least be considered prior to the use of eviction. Particularly where the local authority is also the landlord, consideration should be given to whether and to what extent any failure to fulfil these duties is contributing to the neighbour nuisance problem.

3.2.1 Byelaws and Management Orders

Local authorities have the power to make byelaws 'for the management, use and regulation of houses held by them for housing purposes' [1]. Byelaws may not be made which serve to duplicate other statutory legislation, or which contravene the general law [2]. Local authorities may also make 'management rules' for the regulation of the use of, and the conduct of persons while in or on, any land or premises owned or controlled by the [3]. Whereas failure to comply with a byelaw may be an offence, punishable by a fine [4], the sanction for contravention of a management order is expulsion or exclusion from the land or premises [5]. All local authorities must keep public registers of their byelaws and management orders available for inspection free of charge [6].

[1] Housing (Scotland) Act 1987, section 18. Entitlement to make byelaws also exists in the Local Government (Scotland) Act 1973, section 201 as amended by Schedule 13 to the Local Government etc (Scotland) Act 1994. On byelaws and management orders generally, see *Stair Memorial Encyclopaedia*, Vol. 14, paragraphs 269–301. The introduction of a range of offences for public order offences in the Civic Government (Scotland) Act 1982 has reduced the need for byelaws in housing matters. See, for example, the Home Office Model 'Noise' byelaw, reproduced in Penn 'Noise Control: the law and its enforcement' (1995), page 78.

[2] 1973 Act, section 210(3); *Kerr v Hood* 1907 SC 895.

[3] Civic Government (Scotland) Act 1982, section 112.

[4] Unless otherwise specified in the statute under which the byelaw is made, the penalty for summary conviction of breach of a byelaw is a fine not exceeding level 2 on the standard scale (currently £500.00) with a further daily penalty of £5.00 for ongoing failure to comply.

[5] 1982 Act, sections 116, 117.

[6] 1982 Act, section 115.

3.2.2 Local Government (Scotland) Act 1973, section 189

This provides that where a local authority considers it 'expedient for the promotion or protection of the interests of the inhabitants of their area or any part thereof, they may institute, defend or appear in any legal proceedings'. It is thought that this does not give any general right to bring prosecutions in criminal matters, even in relation to byelaws [1].

[1] See paragraph 3.1.1,n2 above.

3.2.3 Mental Health and Care in the Community [1]

3.2.3.1 It is thought that the increase in neighbour nuisance complaints is at least partly a consequence of the policy of closing psychiatric hospitals and rehousing former inpatients in the community. Although such a policy has clear advantages for some patients, present reports suggest a shortage of resources is leading to failures of care in practice. This in turn can lead to a wide range of behavioural and health problems, difficulties with maintaining a tenancy, and tension with neighbours. Unfortunately this situation is worsened by sensationalist media coverage of particular criminal or violent patients. This leads to fear, suspicion and prejudice to many sufferers. The question for social landlords must be whether and to what extent the alleged anti-social behaviour has a 'community care/mental health element' and whether and to what extent that behaviour has been caused or exacerbated by failings on the part of the local authority to fulfil its duties under the relevant law [2].

[1] On the law relating to mental health see Blackie and Patrick *Mental Health: a guide to the law in Scotland* (now out of print, and rather out of date – a second edition is believed to be in preparation). On community care law, see McKay and Patrick *The Care Maze* (1995) Enable/SAMH.

[2] For example, a failure to have in place practical after-care arrangements, including accommodation and appropriate support for a patient leaving a psychiatric hospital – and to do so before discharge: see, for example, *R v Ealing District Health Authority, ex parte F* [1993] 1 WLR 373; [1993] 3 All ER 170; *The Times*, 24th June 1992.

3.2.3.2   Local authority duties towards patients receiving care in the community are contained in the Social Work (Scotland) Act 1968 (as amended by the National Health Service and Community Care Act 1990), particularly sections 12, 12A and 14, the Mental Health (Scotland) Act 1984, particularly sections 7, 8 and 11, the Disabled Persons (Services, Consultation and Representation) Act 1986 and the Chronically Sick and Disabled Persons Act 1970. There is also a mass of official guidance on every aspect of community care, which is constantly updated [1]. In broad terms, these provisions oblige a local authority (in practice the social work department) to assess a persons need for social work services and to draw up a care plan for that individual, with the principal aim being to provide such services as will enable the person to live a normal life within the community.

[1] Local authorities must act in accordance with this guidance – 1968 Act, section 5. A failure to do so may render its acting unlawful: *R v Yorkshire Council, ex parte Hargreaves, The Times*, 9th November 1994. The guidance is available free of charge from the Social Work Services Group, 43 Jeffrey Street, Edinburgh. See in particular SW7/1994 *Community Care: the housing dimension*; SW11/1991 *Assessment and Care Management*; and SW1992/1 *Guidance on Care Programmes for People with a Mental Illness, including Dementia*.

3.2.3.3 Powers to compulsorily admit or recall to hospital persons suffering from mental disorder are contained in the Mental Health (Scotland) Act 1984 (as amended). Applications for compulsory admission are generally initiated by the mental health officer (usually a social worker appointed by the local authority) [1], although emergency admissions may be made on the certification of a general medical practitioner [2]. A person may be compulsorily admitted to hospital only where s/he is suffering from a mental disorder of a nature or degree which makes it appropriate for him or her to receive medical treatment in hospital [3]. It must also be necessary for his or her health or safety, or for the protection of other people, that s/he should receive such treatment, and it must be the case that it cannot be provided unless the person is detained. A person detained can be required to take medication for their mental disorder [4]. Persons detained may be given (renewable) leave of absence at the discretion of the hospital's responsible medical officer [5]. Such leave may be revoked at any time, unless the criteria for admission are not judged to be met on that date [6].

[1] 1984 Act, section 9. Applications for admission are made to the sheriff court under detailed procedure outlined in sections 18–21 of the Act. If approved, the person may be detained for up to six months, which period may be renewed for a further six months and annually thereafter.

[2] 1984 Act, section 24. The doctor must certify that it is urgently necessary that the person be admitted, and that following the normal procedure for admission would involve undesirable delay. An emergency admission lasts 72 hours, although this may be extended by a further 28 days under section 26. In practice, this form of compulsory admission is far more common than the section 18 procedure. There is no right of appeal against a section 24 detention. Appeal is available against a 28-day detention, but in practical terms only the minority of cases are brought before a sheriff for approval.

[3] 1984 Act, section 18. Many persons suffering from mental disorders will not satisfy these criteria, and detention will therefore be inappropriate. Included in this group are persons suffering from personality disorder.

[4] 1984 Act, Part X.

[5] 1984 Act, section 27. Persons on leave of absence can still be required to take medication. Two issues are currently controversial in practice. The first is the extent to which patients are placed on leave of absence as a direct result of a shortage of hospital beds. The second is the degree to which persons on leave of absence have this leave renewed without proper consideration being given to whether they are still detainable.

[6] 1984 Act, section 27(6). Note also section 35A of the 1984 Act (as inserted by the Patients in the Community Act 1995). A patient may only be placed on leave of absence for 12 months. Thereafter if not to be detained in hospital or discharged, he can be made the subject of a Community Care Order, restricting/regulating his life outside hospital. Such an order cannot require him to take medication against his will.

3.2.4 Planning and Building Controls

3.2.4.1 Planning authorities possess substantial regulatory powers to deal with development [1]. 'Development' includes not only the carrying out of building and engineering operations (including alterations and demolitions) but also the making of a material change of use of land and buildings [2]. Thus, an occupier who begins to operate a business from his home may have therefore materially changed the use of the house and require planning permission. The change of use of a house so that it comprises two or more separate dwellings constitutes development [3]. Other matters constituting 'development' include the depositing of refuse or waste materials on land and certain external advertisements [4]. Where a person wishes to undertake development (within the meaning of the legislation) s/he must obtain planning permission. If permission is refused, there is a right of appeal to the Secretary of State [5].

[1] For more detail of the law relating to planning controls, see Henderson (1989) *Scottish Planning Sourcebook* (and Updates) Hillside Publishing; Henderson and O'Carroll (1994) *Town and Country Planning in Scotland: Powers and Procedures*, Hillside Publishing; Young and Rowan Robinson (1985) *Scottish Planning Law and Procedure*, Hodge; Collar (1994) *Planning*, Greens/Sweet & Maxwell; McAllister and McMaster (1994) *Scottish Planning Law*, Butterworths.

[2] Town and Country Planning (Scotland) Act 1972, section 19.

[3] 1972 Act, section 19(3). However, the keeping of lodgers does not constitute change of use providing there are not more than five residents in all – Use Classes Order 1989 (SI 1989/147). Other activities run from home which may constitute a material change of use and thus development could include provision of a taxi service or using a domestic garage for car repairs or other industry.

[4] 1972 Act, section 19(3); 1972 Act, section 61 and Control of Advertisements (Scotland) Regulations 1984 (SI 1984/1467) as amended by SI 1992/1763.

[5] 1972 Act, section 33.

3.2.4.2 Where unauthorised development has taken place, or where there is a failure to comply with a planning condition, the planning authority has a variety of enforcement mechanisms. Breach of planning control is not usually a criminal offence. Planning authorities have discretion to take enforcement action against a breach of planning control if they consider such action to be expedient 'having regard to the development plan and any other material considerations' [1]. Where a breach of a planning condition is involved, the planning authority may issue a breach of condition notice requiring compliance [2]. In addition, and in any other case, the planning authority may serve an enforcement notice requiring specified action to be taken to discontinue the breach within a specified period [3]. A stop notice may be issued in addition to an enforcement notice where the planning authority consider it expedient that any 'relevant activity' should cease before the expiry of the period of time specified in the enforcement notice [4]. The planning authority has powers to seek interdict and interim interdict to prevent a continuing or threatened breach of planning controls [5]. Finally, the planning authority has the power to enter on land to carry out required works, if not undertaken by the person on whom the relevant notice has been served, at the expense of the owner or lessee [6].

[1]   Town and Country Planning (Scotland) Act 1972, section 84 (as amended by the Planning and Compensation Act 1991).

[2]   1972 Act, section 87AA (inserted by the 1991 Act). Failure to comply is a criminal offence.

[3]   1972 Act, sections 84 and 84AA (inserted by the 1991 Act). Failure to comply is a criminal offence: 1972 Act, section 86 (as amended by the 1991 Act).

[4]   1972 Act, section 87 (as amended by the 1991 Act).

[5]   1972 Act, section 260A (inserted by the 1991 Act).

[6]   1972 Act, section 88 (as amended by the 1991 Act).

3.2.5   Children

A perhaps surprising proportion of neighbour nuisance appears to be directly caused by children [1]. Given the battery of legal powers available to local authorities in relation to children, it should be only in extreme circumstances that eviction of an entire family as a result of a child's conduct can be considered an appropriate remedy [2].

[1]   See e.g. *Glenrothes Development Corporation v Graham* (unrep.) 14th December 1994, Kirkcaldy Sheriff Court, Sheriff Patrick, paragraph 10.2.3.10 below; *Dundee District Council v Anderson* (unrep.) 8th September 1993, Dundee Sheriff Court, Sheriff MacFarlane; 3rd February 1995, Dundee Sheriff Court, Sheriff Principal Maguire, paragraph 8.15.2 below; *Midlothian District Council v Tweedie* (unrep.) 3rd March 1993, Edinburgh Sheriff Court, Sheriff Principal Nicholson; 1993 GWD 16-1068, paragraph 7.3.3, etc.

[2]   See generally Part II of the Children (Scotland) Act 1955; *Stair Memorial Encyclopaedia,* Vol. 22, paragraph 17; Norrie *Children (Scotland) Act 1995* (Greens annotated statutes); Kearney (1987)*Childrens Hearings and the Sheriff Court* (Butterworths); Norrie (1997) *Children's Hearings in Scotland* (Greens/Sweet & Maxwell).

3.3 Neighbour Nuisance: Criminal Offences

This section outlines the main offences that may be of relevance in a neighbour nuisance situation. The intention is simply to provide a checklist (particularly of less well known and statutory offences), rather than a detailed account of the law relating to each offence. It should also be clear, in addition, that whatever the cause of neighbour nuisance, a lack of laws prohibiting it is not one of them.

3.3.1 Assault

An assault is any deliberate attack on the person of another, and may include even minor attacks such as spitting or slapping. Actual injury to the victim is not necessary (although that must have been the intention), nor that there has been physical contact: an attempt to strike with a weapon or fist will be an assault if it merely causes alarm and apprehension. It is enough to menace someone by brandishing a weapon at them thereby putting them into fear of actual injury [1].

[1] See Gordon, paragraphs 29–01 *et seq.*

3.3.2 Threats

Threatening a person with death, grievous bodily harm, or serious injury to 'property, fortune or reputation' is a criminal offence in itself [1]. This includes written threats such as those contained in 'poison pen letters'. Lesser threats which may put the recipient into a state of fear or alarm may constitute a breach of the peace if the alarm is objectively 'caused or reasonably to be apprehended' [2]; so may insults likely to provoke a violent reaction [3].

[1] *Jas Miller* (1862) 4 Irv. 238; Gordon, paragraph 29–61.

[2] Gordon, paragraph 29–63.

[3] *Stair Memorial Encyclopaedia*,Vol. 7, paragraph 454.

3.3.3 Breach of the Peace

Virtually any conduct causing public disturbance can amount to a breach of the peace at common law [1], including kerb crawling, or being a 'peeping tom'. There is authority to the effect that a breach of the peace can even be committed in private [2] but this is unlikely to be the case in general. A noisy party taking place in a private house but heard outside the house may be a breach, however [3].

[1] 'Typically a breach of the peace is a public disturbance, such as brawling or fighting in public, shouting and swearing in the street, or any general tumult or interference with the peace of a neighbourhood. Whether any particular acts amount to such a disturbance is a question of fact depending on the circumstances of each case, and strictly speaking probably no case on breach of the peace can be regarded as an authority of general application': Gordon, *Criminal Law* (Greens 1978), paragraph 41–01. In *R v Howell* [1981] 3 All ER 383 it was held that there is a breach of the peace whenever harm is actually done, or is likely to be done to someone, or where harm is done in that persons presence to his property, or where a person is in fear of being harmed through an assault, affray, riot, unlawful assembly or other disturbance.

[2] *Young v Heatley* 1959 JC 66.

[3] *Ferguson v Carnochan* (1889) 2 White 278; Gordon, paragraph 41–10.

3.3.4 Harassment

While there is no specific offence of harassment in Scotland, it is thought that the common law relating to assaults, threats and breach of the peace is sufficiently broad to permit possible prosecution of all behaviour which might commonly be called 'harassment' [1].

[1] In England, where the common law is thought to be weaker in this regard, statutory offences of harassment have been created: Public Order Act 1986, sections 4 and 5. These have recently been added to in an attempt to deal with racial harassment in particular: 1986 Act, section 4A(1) (as introduced by the Criminal Justice and Public Order Act 1994, section 154). None of these statutory offences apply to Scotland. Note however the new power to bring an action of damages for harassment, to obtain interdict or interim interdict or a 'non-harassment order': Protection from Harassment Act 1997 sections 8–11.

3.3.5 Racial Harassment

There is no specific offence of racial harassment as such, although depending on its form such behaviour may constitute the crime of assault, breach of the peace etc. Inciting others to such behaviour is, however, prohibited by statute. The Public Order Act 1986 provides that a person who uses threatening, abusive or insulting words or behaviour, or displays any written material of such character is guilty of a criminal offence if he intends to stir up racial hatred and if that is likely to be the result of his actions in the circumstances [1]. The offence may be committed in a public or private place, and the police may arrest without warrant anyone reasonably suspected of committing the offence. It is a defence to show that the person did not intend his words or behaviour to be threatening, abusive or insulting, and was not aware that they might be. It is also an offence to publish or distribute written material intending to stir up racial hatred [2] or to be in possession of racially inflammatory material (including video or sound recordings) to the same end [3]. The police have specific powers of search in respect of premises suspected to contain such material [4].

[1] 1986 Act, section 18(1). 'Racial hatred' means hatred against a group defined by reference to colour, race, nationality or ethnic or national origins.

[2] 1986 Act, section 19.

[3] 1986 Act, section 23.

[4] 1986 Act, section 24(2).

3.3.6 Damage to Property

3.3.6.1 Malicious Mischief

It is a crime at common law to destroy or damage the property of another person, or to interfere with it to the detriment of the owner or lawful possessor [1]. For the crime to be committed, the destruction must be wilful (either intentional or reckless), although there is no requirement that it be spiteful. It may be that it is not necessary even for physical damage to be caused, if financial loss has been caused [2].

[1] Gordon *Criminal Law* (2nd edition), paragraph 22.01.

[2] *HMA v Wilson* 1983 SCCR 420.

3.3.6.2 Vandalism

It is a statutory offence to wilfully or recklessly destroy or damagg, without reasonable excuse, any property belonging to another person [1]. This would appear to add little to the common law of malicious mischief, although the limits to the penalties for vandalism are set by statute [2]. 'Reasonable excuse' must be considered objectively and in the light of all the circumstances [3].

[1] Criminal Law (Consolidation) (Scotland) Act 1995, section 52(1).

[2] 1995 Act, section 52(3).

[3] In *MacDougall v Ho* 1985 SCCR 199, the accused was acquitted of vandalism after breaking the windscreen of a car, after it was established that the car contained persons wrongly but genuinely believed to have damaged the accuseds shop.

3.3.6.3 Damage to local authority housing

It is an offence to damage local authority housing [1]. In particular the offence is committed when a person (not necessarily the tenant) 'wilfully or by culpable negligence' damages or suffers to be damaged either the house, its fittings or its appurtenances. This includes the drainage, water supply or fencing of the house. The maximum fine for such damage is £50.00, although the local authority's right to seek compensation is reserved.

[1] Housing (Scotland) Act 1987, section 320.

3.3.7 Weapons

It is an offence to be in possession of an offensive weapon in a public place [1]. There is no closed list of what may constitute a 'weapon', but three categories are distinguished: those articles which are designed for causing injury (for example a gun); those which are adapted to cause injury (for example a sharpened screwdriver) and those which are not offensive weapons at all but for the intention of the person carrying them to use them as such (for example a piece of wood or baseball bat). Although it is a defence to show a 'reasonable excuse' for carrying a weapon, this is construed very narrowly by the courts: it is not, for example, a reasonable excuse to carry a weapon in 'self defence'. Carrying a knife (or other sharp pointed or bladed instrument) in a public place is generally an offence [2]. It is not necessary to prove intention on the part of the accused: the carrying of the knife in itself constitutes the crime [3].

[1] Criminal Law (Consolidation) (Scotland) Act 1995, section 47.

[2] 1995 Act, section 49.

[3] It remains a defence to show good reason for carrying the knife, or to be able to show that the knife is for work, religious purposes or as part of national costume. It is unlikely that anything but a restrictive interpretation on such a defence will be provided by the courts. Forgetting to dispose of the knife after the good reason has ceased will not be a defence – *Lister v Lees* 1994 SLT 1328, 1994 SCCR 548.

3.3.8 Noise: Criminal Offences

3.3.8.1 Any person who sings, performs, plays a musical instrument or any form of hi-fi, so as to give any other person reasonable cause for annoyance, and who fails to stop when asked to do so by a uniformed police constable, is guilty of a criminal offence [1]. This need not be in a public place. Such conduct may in any event involve a breach of the peace [2].

[1] Civic Government (Scotland) Act 1982, section 54(1). The fine, on summary conviction, may not exceed £50.00. The offence is not, of course, committed if the person making the noise stops doing so when asked.

[2] *Hughes v Crowe* 1993 SCCR 320.

3.3.8.2 Breach of a noise abatement notice or order is a criminal offence and may give rise to prosecution and fine [1].

[1] See paragraph 6.2.2.5 below.

3.3.8.3 The police probably have the power to remove any articles being used in the commission of an offence. This would include hi-fis or other noise-making instruments being used in a breach of the peace [1]. The court is empowered to entertain motions for forfeiture of property used or intended to be used for the purpose of committing or facilitating the commission of any offence. Such a motion may be entertained on conviction or where the accused is the subject of an absolute discharge in summary or district court proceedings. There seems no reason why sound generating equipment should not fall within this definition in the appropriate case [2]. That there is uncertainty about the extent of police powers in this area is in itself a reason for statutory clarification [3].

[1] Or an offence under section 54 of the 1982 Act. This power of the police to confiscate does not apparently exist in England and Wales. See, however, Chapter 6 below (especially paragraph 6.2) – where a noise abatement notice has not been complied with, some local authorities have taken the view that they are empowered to enter premises and confiscate noise-making equipment under the powers contained in the Environmental Protection Act 1990 (section 81(3); Schedule 3, paragraph 2). For an example of the use of this power in confiscating sound equipment from anti-social tenants, see *Environmental Health News*, 31st January 1992, page 7.

[2] Proceeds of Crime (Scotland) Act 1995 Part II and see annotations to this Act by AL Brown (1995) Greens/Sweet & Maxwell.

[3] See Report of Scottish Affairs Grand Committee on Housing and Anti-Social Behaviour Cmnd. 196 (1996).

3.3.8.4 Parties and Raves

Although the police now have extensive powers to regulate raves, these powers are unlikely to have relevance in neighbour dispute situations [1]. There are no particular offences directed towards the holding of domestic parties as such.

[1] Criminal Justice and Public Order Act 1994, section 63 – although applicable to Scotland, these provisions only relate to open air parties where 100 or more persons attend, and where rave music (as defined!) is played so as to cause serious distress to local inhabitants.

3.3.9 Drugs

Insofar as drug taking takes place in private and outwith the sight and sound of neighbours, it is debatable whether it constitutes 'anti-social' behaviour on the part of an occupier at all. More frequently the complaint from the neighbour will turn on either the behaviour of the drug user whilst under the influence, or the use of the house to sell drugs, leading, for example, to frequent casual visitors late at night etc. [1]. In particular, an offence is committed if the occupier of premises permits the production or supply of controlled drugs, or the smoking of certain drugs, in the premises occupied [2]. A co-tenant may be convicted of permitting another co-tenant to use the premises to break the law in this way [3], but a casual visitor is not to be regarded as an 'occupier' for this purpose [4].

[1] Prescribed drugs are controlled by the Misuse of Drugs Act 1971.

[2] 1971 Act, section 8. Conviction for the use of a house for immoral or illegal purposes is a ground for eviction: see paragraphs 10.4.1, 11.1.4 and 11.2.2 below.

[3] *R v Ashdown* (1974) 59 Cr App R 193.

[4] *R v Mogford* [1970] 1 WLR 988.

3.3.10 Control of Animals and Criminal Offences

Dogs and other animals regularly feature in neighbour nuisance cases. The following sections relate to the regulation and use of animals rather than questions of civil liability which may arise from damage caused by them [1].

[1] There is a surprising amount of law on animals and on dogs in particular. For further information see *Stair Memorial Encyclopaedia*, Vol. 2. See also G Sandys-Winsch (1993), *The Dog Law Handbook*, Shaw & Sons which, although an English law text, is both exhaustive and informative.

3.3.10.1 Licensing of Dogs

There is no requirement to have a licence for a dog kept for purposes other than breeding [1]. Breeding or rearing dogs from a domestic house without local authority licensing is, however, an offence [2]. The Act applies to premises where two or more bitches are kept for the purpose of breeding for sale, or where puppies are kept for rearing or sale [3].

[1] Local Government Act 1988, section 41, Schedule 7, repealing the Dog Licensing Act 1959, as amended. The Secretary of State retains the power to introduce a dog licensing or registration scheme, but the previous government declared their intention not to do so: 1988 Act, section 37; Hansard, HC Vol. 129, col. 452.

[2] Breeding of Dogs Act 1973, section 5(1), as amended by the Civic Government (Scotland) Act 1982, section 137 and Schedule 3, paragraph 3(9). A specific exemption may, however, apply: Animal Health Act 1981. Such licences must be renewed annually: 1973 Act, sections 1(6), (7).

[3] 1973 Act, section 5(2).

3.3.10.2 Collaring of Dogs

All dogs must be collared whilst on a highway or in a 'place of public resort'. Failure to do so is a criminal offence and the dog may be seized by the police or local authority and treated as a stray [1].

[1] Animal Health Act 1981, section 13, as amended by the Environmental Protection Act 1990, section 151; Control of Dogs Order 1992, SI 1992/901. These provisions may be executed and enforced by officers of the local authority as well as the police.

3.3.10.3 Fouling by Dogs

It is an offence to permit a dog to foul the footpath, grass verge, pedestrian precinct, children's play area or recreation area [1].

[1] Civic Government (Scotland) Act 1982, section 48(1). This matter is also regulated by byelaws: see *Westminster City Council v Harris* [1990] NLJ 1063; Alldridge: *Incontinent Dogs and the Law* [1990] NLJ 1067. See also the Environmental Protection Act 1990, section 86(14); Litter (Animal Droppings) Order 1991, SI 1991/961, applying the provisions of Part IV of the 1990 Act to dog excrement deposited in certain public places. In terms of section 87(4), a person guilty of the offence of littering may be liable for a fine of up to £2,500.00.

3.3.10.4 Dangerous Dogs

Any police officer may take possession of any dog that s/he has reason to suppose to be savage or dangerous, straying on any highway and not under the control of any person [1]. The dog may be the subject of a complaint to the sheriff, who, if s/he finds that it is dangerous and not under proper control, may make an order requiring the owner to take specified measures to keep the dog under proper control, or alternatively that the dog should be destroyed [2]. It is irrelevant that the dog may not have hurt anyone [3].

[1] Dogs Act 1871, section 1. 'Dangerous' means 'savage or ferocious'. It relates to the nature and disposition of the dog itself, not what it does. Accordingly it may be 'dangerous' to other animals or property, as well as humans: *Henderson v Mackenzie* (1876) 3 R 623.

[2] 1871 Act, section 2. The conditions may include muzzling the dog or neutering it: Dangerous Dogs Act 1991, sections 5(b), 6. The proceedings are not those to which the criminal ('beyond reasonable doubt') standard of proof applies: *Anderson v Guild* 1989 GWD 24-1012. Where a court makes an order under section 2, it may also require delivery of the dog, and appoint a person to destroy it, and alternatively make an order disqualifying the owner from keeping dogs for any specified period: 1871 Act, section 2 as amended by Dangerous Dogs Act 1989, section 1(1). Failure to comply with a section 2 order with regard to controlling or delivering a dog is an offence, which can lead to a fine and disqualification from keeping a dog: 1989 Act, section 1(3). More serious fines can be imposed for contravention of a disqualification order: 1989 Act, section 1(5).

[3] Dangerous Dogs Act 1991, section 5(a).

3.3.10.5 It is an offence to possess certain breeds of fighting dogs [1].

[1] Dangerous Dogs Act 1991. To date these include the pit bull terrier, the Japanese tosa, dogo Argentino, and fila Braziliero: 1991 Act section 1(1); Dangerous Dogs (Designated Types) Order 1991, SI 1991/1743. Unless an exemption applies, it is an offence to possess such a dog, to the extent of up to six months in prison or a fine: 1991 Act, section 1(3), (5), (7). The onus is on the owner to prove that the dog is not of the prohibited breed: *Scott v Heywood* 1993 GWD 3-142, *Simpson v Lees* 1992 GWD 31-1796. The test is in relation to the characteristics of the dog rather than its strict pedigree, or whether it is full or half breed: *Parker v Annan* 1994 SLT 675, 1993 SCCR 185; *Annan v Troup* 1994 SLT 679, 1993 SCCR 192.

3.3.10.6 If a dog is dangerously out of control [1] in a public place [2], the owner or person in charge of it will be guilty of a criminal offence. If by being dangerously out of control , the dog causes injury to another person, then a more severe fine can be imposed than otherwise [3], and the sheriff has no discretion but to order the destruction of the dog [4].

[1] 1991 Act, section 3. What is meant by being 'dangerously out of control' will depend on the particular circumstances. For example, a dog will not be out of control simply because it bites someone, but might be if it is then allowed to bite again: compare *Normand v Lucas* 1993 GWD 15–975 with *Tierney v Valentine* 1994 SCCR 697. The police can obtain a warrant to enter premises and seize a dangerous dog: 1991 Act, section 5. Criminal liability extends to the parent or guardian where the dog is owned or controlled by a person under the age of sixteen years: 1991 Act, section 6.

[2] The 1991 Act defines 'public place' as a place to which the public has access, including the common parts of a building which has two or more flats. This will include the common stair or landings in a block of flats or tenements, but not the back green of a 'four in a block' house: *McGeachy v Normand* 1994 SLT 429, 1993 SCCR 951; and possibly not the front garden with the exception of the path: *McGeachy*, supra, disapproving *DPP v Fellowes* 1993 Crim LR 523.

[3] 1991 Act, section 3(4)(a),(b).

[4] *Normand v Freeman* 1992 SLT 598, 1992 SCCR 417.

3.3.10.7 Other Animals

A district court may make an order to control (but not destroy) any creature where that creature is giving a neighbouring resident 'reasonable cause for annoyance' [1]. 'Any person' can apply for such an order, but this will not include a local authority acting either as a public health authority or on behalf of neighbouring residents [2].

[1] Civic Government (Scotland) Act 1982, section 49(2). Failure to comply with such an order is an offence: 1982 Act, section 49(4).

[2] *City of Edinburgh District Council, Petrs* 1990 SCCR 511. The resident or residents in the vicinity of the annoyance must bring the action on their own behalf. There is no right of appeal from such an order: *MacPherson, Petrs* 1990 JC 5, 1989 SCCR 518; *McKay, Petr* (unrep.) 7th July 1989 – noted at 1989 SCCR 524.

3.3.10.8 No person may keep a dangerous wild animal unless licensed to do so by the local authority [1].

[1] Dangerous Wild Animals Act 1976, section 1(1). Failure to comply with this provision is a criminal offence: 1976 Act, section 2(5). The 1976 Act only applies to particular animals including wild dogs and cats, snakes, bears, emus and other exotic species: 1976 Act, section 7(4), (5) and Schedule. If a person contravenes the Act the local authority, and the police, have the power to enter premises, seize the animal and either keep it or destroy it, without obligation to pay compensation to the owner: 1976 Act, section 4(1); *Halpern v Chief Constable of Strathclyde* 1988 SCLR 137.

3.3.11 Littering

If litter amounts to an accumulation of deposit including offensive matter, refuse, offal or manure which is a nuisance or prejudicial to health, then it may be a statutory nuisance [1]. If any person litters a public open place, then a criminal offence is committed [2]. It is possible to convict under this provision on the evidence of one uncorroborated witness [3]. 'Litter' includes inadequately packaged commercial waste, but it will be necessary to show when the material was placed on the street as well as the fact that it had been so placed [4]. Offenders do not, however, need to be reported to the police for prosecution, as 'authorised officers' of the local authority can issue fixed penalty notices [5]. Littering a common stair is also an offence punishable by fine [6].

[1] Environmental Protection Act 1990, section 79(1) for cases decided under the previous leglislation, Public Health (Scotland) Act 1897, section 16(5), see *Gray v Dunlop* 1954 SLT (Sh Ct) 75; *Clydebank District Council v Monaville Estates Ltd* 1982 SLT (Sh Ct) 2. See paragraph 6.2.1.2 below.

[2] Environmental Protection Act 1990, section 87(1), (3). A public open place is any open air place to which the public have free access, including streets and highways: 1990 Act, section 87(4).

[3] 1990 Act, section 87(7).

[4] *Westminster City Council v Riding, The Times,* 31st July 1995, QBD. See also Brown, 'Comment: Waste and Litter' (Greens Environmental Law Bulletin, Issue 9, October 1995) where the Senior Procurator Fiscal Depute in Edinburgh argues that it is the scattering of the litter, rather than the mere placing of it on the street, which creates the offence. In other words, the placing of material on the street, so far ahead of expected collection as to involve significant risk of the tearing of the packaging and scattering of the material will constitute depositing of material in such circumstances as to tend to lead to defacement by litter in terms of the statute, thereby constituting the offence.

[5] I.e. the liability to conviction may be discharged on payment of a fixed penalty fine: 1990 Act, section 88; Litter (Fixed Penalty Notices) Order 1991, SI 1991/111. See also paragraph 3.7.3 below.

[6] Civic Government (Scotland) Act 1982, section 92(9).

3.3.12 Urinating or Defecating

It is a criminal offence to urinate or defecate in a public place so as to cause or to be likely to cause annoyance or nuisance to any other person [1].

[1] Civic Government (Scotland) Act 1982, section 47.

3.3.13 Drunk and Incapable

It is an offence to be drunk and incapable of taking care of oneself in a public place. It is further an offence to be drunk while in charge of a child of under 10 years of age, or to be drunk and in charge of a firearm [1].

[1] Civic Government (Scotland) Act 1982, section 50. 'Public place' means any place to which the public have unrestricted access and includes thoroughfares, doorways and entrances of premises abutting onto a public place, common passages, closes, stairs, garden or yard pertinent to any tenement or group of separately owned houses: 1982 Act, section 133. For the purposes of section 50 of the 1982 Act, 'public place' also includes a place to which the public may have access on payment, and also public transport: 1982 Act, section 50(6). 'Firearm' includes a crossbow or airgun: 1982 Act, section 50(5).

3.3.14 Obstruction

It is an offence to wilfully obstruct the passage of another person in a public place, or to act with others in doing so and refusing to stop when required to do so by the police [1].

[1] Civic Government (Scotland) Act 1982, section 53. On meaning of 'public place', see paragraph 3.3.13 above.

3.3.15 Fire Lighting

It is an offence to lay or light a fire in a public place so as to endanger any other person or give them reasonable cause for alarm [1].

[1] Civic Government (Scotland) Act 1982, section 56. On meaning of 'public place' see paragraph 3.3.13 above.

3.3.16 Malicious and Obscene Communications

A person who uses the public telephone system to send a message that is either grossly offensive, indecent, obscene or menacing, or who sends false messages in order to cause annoyance, inconvenience or needless anxiety, is guilty of an offence [1] punishable by a fine or imprisonment [2]. A person who sends a letter or postal packet either enclosing or displaying on the outside any indecent or obscene matter or communication is guilty of an offence [3]. It is further an offence to send unsolicited material describing or illustrating human sexual techniques [4].

[1] Telecommunications Act 1984, section 43.

[2] Criminal Justice and Public Order Act 1994, section 92: imprisonment may be for a period of up to six months and the fine may be up to £5,000.00.

[3] Post Office Act 1953, section 11(1). 'Indecent or obscene' means shocking or lewd. (n.b. the Malicious Communications Act 1988 does not apply to Scotland).

[4] Unsolicited Goods and Services Act 1971, section 4.

3.3.17 Cleaning of Common Areas

It is the duty of the occupiers of houses or flats with access or rights in common to use common areas, to keep those areas clean and decorated to the satisfaction of the local authority [1]. The authority may make byelaws to regulate cleaning of common property and failure to comply with such a byelaw may lead to summary conviction and fine.

[1] Civic Government (Scotland) Act 1982, section 92(2).

3.3.18 Prostitution

A prostitute, whether male or female, who either loiters in a public place or solicits so as to be seen from a public place (for example, from a window of a house), or importunes a person who is in a public place is guilty of an offence [1]. A person soliciting or importuning on behalf of a prostitute will also be guilty of an offence [2]. Managing or assisting in the management of a house as a brothel is an offence, as is permitting all or part of premises to be used as such [3]. A house will not, however, be a brothel simply because one prostitute lives there and he or she alone uses it for trade [4].

[1] Civic Government (Scotland) Act 1982, section 46. In order to be convicted of importuning, it must be established that the person is a prostitute on evidence other than that connected with the present charge. On prostitution and brothel-keeping generally, see Gordon, paragraphs 36.25–36.48.

[2] Criminal Law (Consolidation) (Scotland) Act 1995, section 11(1).

[3] 1995 Act, section 11(5). This includes permission by the tenant, and not just a landlord. Conviction for use of the house for immoral or illegal purposes can found an action for eviction. See paragraphs 10.4.1 and 11.1.2 below.

[4] *Singleton v Ellison* [1895] 1 QB 607.

4 INTERDICT AND INTERIM INTERDICT

Where anti-social conduct threatens or infringes personal or property rights, the wrongdoer may be restrained by an interdict. Social landlords in Scotland are increasingly using this remedy as the first legal step against tenants causing nuisance and annoyance. There must be an actionable wrong and title for the landlord to sue. The procedure can be quicker and more efficient than seeking recovery of possession.

4.1 An interdict [1] is an order from the court prohibiting a person or persons from carrying out some act which they are legally bound not to do. It is a means to prevent a wrong from happening in the future, rather than to give redress for a wrong already committed [2]. This may be either a particular wrong yet to occur (for example, a noisy party), or a continuation of a wrongful act which has already begun (for example, using the front yard to run a noisy car repair business) [3]. The anticipated act must in fact be a 'wrong'. In general, this will occur where either property or personal rights are infringed or threatened [4]. Those rights may exist in terms of the criminal law, the common law of nuisance, the lease, or (where the wrongdoer is an owner-occupier) the burdens and conditions of title.

[1] Comprehensive textbooks are available on its nature: Burn Murdoch on *Interdict* (1933); S. Scott Robinson *The Law of Interdict* (1994) and procedure: MacPhail, *Sheriff Court Practice,* paragraphs 21.72–21.88. Our purpose here, however, is to highlight those aspects of interdict relevant to its use as a legal remedy by landlords against anti-social tenants.

[2] *Earl of Breadalbane v Jamieson* (1877) 4 R 667 at 671.

[3] *Inverurie Magistrates v Sorrie* 1956 SLT (N) 17, 1956 SC 175 at 179.

[4] See D.M. Walker, *Civil Remedies* (Greens 1975), page 227; *Winans v Macrae* (1885) 12 R 1051 at 1063.

4.2 The use of interdict is gaining acceptance by some Scottish social landlords as an alternative to repossession as a method of dealing with tenants causing nuisance and annoyance [1]. In England, injunctions (the English equivalent of interdicts) have been extensively used by a number of public landlords, notably Salford City Council and Manchester City Council [2]. In Scotland, Dundee District Council has instituted a policy of seeking interdicts against allegedly anti-social tenants. Apparently on only one occasion has this council been unsuccessful in obtaining a court order [3].

Interdicts have not always been successful in remedying the conduct, but the policy is proving sufficiently successful to justify its continuation. Edinburgh District Council has also employed interdict to deal with the problem. A study of their use has found that interdict is a useful management tool in some circumstances [4]. The landlord is not barred from seeking interdict merely because he has the alternative remedy of bringing possession proceedings [5]. In addition, interdicts can be directed at the landlord's tenants, the tenant's resident family, and other occupiers who either own their own houses or are tenants of other landlords.

[1] The use of interdict as a first legal weapon against anti-social tenants has much to commend it. It is speedy, less drastic than eviction and can be selectively directed at the guilty persons rather than any innocent co-residents.

[2] Aldbourne Associates (1993) *Managing Neighbour Complaints in Social Housing: A Handbook for Practitioners,* page 30.

[3] Out of 24 cases brought by the council to June 1995. Most difficulties apparently arise in relation to breaches of the interdicts rather than obtaining the orders in the first place.

[4] See paragraph 4.10 below.

[5] See, for example, *Sutton Housing Trust v Lawrence* (1987) 19 HLR 520. Indeed it can seek both remedies simultaneously (see, for example, *Basildon District Council v Mills* (unrep.) 27th September 1994, Brentwood County Court, LAG, March 1995, page 11) or in some unusual circumstances in the same action (see paragraph 8.3 below).

4.3 Interdict: Title and Interest to Sue

In order for a landlord to bring an action for interdict against anti-social behaviour, he must establish title and interest to sue. 'He must be a party to some legal relationship which gives him some right which the person against whom he raises the action either infringes or denies'. [1] In the case of *McEwen v Steedman & McAlister* [2], it was held that the landlord had title and interest to sue where the working of a gas engine led to structural damage to the subjects of let and nuisance and annoyance to the occupants. It was observed that the landlord has title to sue a third party for interdict where that party's operations are such as to lower the letting value of his property. On this authority a landlord could seek interdict against *any* person (whether a tenant of his or not) guilty of anti-social behaviour against his tenant. In *Dundee District Council v Cook* [3], however, Sheriff Principal Maguire took a different view, holding that the observations concerning letting values in *McEwen* related to damage to the property, and not personal behaviour towards the tenants [4].

[1] *D & J Nicol v Dundee Harbour Trustees* 1915 SC (HL) 7 at 12-13.

[2] 1912 SC 156 at 163, 164.

[3] 1995 SCLR (N) 559.

[4] An appeal to the Court of Session was marked but dropped. It is suggested that it is incorrectly decided. In *McEwan*, Lord Salvessen in particular noted that it was established that there were two separate grounds for interdict: damage to the property itself, and damage to the tenants in respect of 'material discomfort and annoyance'. It seems curious to attribute his opinion on title to sue to one ground and not the other. In any event (*per* Lord Dundas at 163) '...The point seems at best to be a technical one, for I suppose it might have been got over, if necessary, by inducing one or more of the tenants to lend their names, upon security as to expenses, as pursuers of the action'.

4.4 Where the anti-social behaviour is threatened or perpetrated by a tenant in breach of a nuisance clause of the lease, the landlord has title to sue, as party to the contract of lease. Alternatively, where damage to the structure of the house is threatened, the landlord will have title independent of the lease obligations [1]. The landlord may join with the tenant in bringing the interdict action [2], but is not bound to do so. There is nothing to stop the tenant suing for interdict on his own behalf, both against wrongs directed at his person, and those directed at the subjects of let [3]. Neighbours of anti social tenants cannot, however, interdict the landlord in order to force him to restrain them [4].

[1] *D & J Nicol v Dundee Harbour Trustees,* supra at pages 12–13*; Harvie v Robertson* (1903) 5 F 338; Burn Murdoch on *Interdict, paragraph* 47.

[2] *Jolly v Brown* (1828) 6 S 872.

[3] *Fleming v Gemill* 1908 SC 340.

[4] *Smith v Scott* [1973] Ch 314: unless the landlord has expressly or impliedly authorised the nuisance.

4.5 Actionable Wrongs

4.5.1 Common Law Nuisance

Common law nuisance is any conduct which causes 'serious disturbance or substantial inconvenience to a neighbour or material damage to his property' [1], or 'whatever is intolerably offensive to individuals in their dwelling houses, or inconsistent with the comfort of life' [2]. This does not mean trivial behaviour: 'it must be accepted that a certain amount of inconvenience, annoyance, disturbance and even damage must be accepted as the price ... [one] ... pays for staying ... in a city tenement' [3]. Accordingly the results of the behaviour must be more than just 'sentimental, speculative, trivial discomfort or personal annoyance' [4].

[1] *Watt v Jamieson* 1954 SC 56 at 58; Burn Murdoch on *Interdict,* paragraph 219.

[2] Bells *Principles,* paragraph 974.

[3] *Watt v Jamieson,* supra, page 58.

[4] *Fleming v Hislop* (1886) 13 R (HL) 43 at 45.

4.5.2 The seriousness of the conduct should be looked at in the light of the general social conditions in the neighbourhood: 'close proximity may make that a nuisance which may cease to be so at a distance; and the habit and practice of the neighbourhood has also some weight' [1]. Accordingly. what is acceptable in one set of circumstances may be a nuisance in another [2]. Because nuisance stems from the effects of actions upon the complainer, not the actions themselves, it is possible to interdict a nuisance committed by several persons, even although the particular acts of each individual defender would in themselves not amount to a nuisance [3].

[1] *Inglis v Shotts Iron Co* (1881) 8 R 1006 at 1021.

[2] *Maguire v M'Neil Ltd* 1922 SC 174. Compare with the approach in *Woking Borough Council v Bistram* (1995) 27 HLR 1 and *Dundee District Council v Heggie* (unrep.) 14th January 1991, Dundee Sheriff Court, Sheriff Stewart: see paragraphs 10.2.3.4 and 12.5 below.

[3] *Duke of Buccleuch v Cowan* (1886) 5 M 214 at 216.

4.5.3 Noise Nuisance

At common law [1], it is the level [2] and frequency of the noise [3] which are important, not the specific source. Excessive noise may therefore be a nuisance, even if only periodic [4], but continuous noise at a lower level may not. For example, in *Ball v Ray* [5] it was observed not to be a nuisance to have to endure

'the noise of a piano forte from a neighbour's house or the noise of a neighbour's children in their nursery, which are noises we must reasonably expect, and must to a considerable extent put up with ... [as opposed to a noise which] materially disturbs the comfort of the ... dwelling house and prevents people from sleeping at night.'

An anti-social and unruly tenant and his family were interdicted in *Smith v Scott* supra, for 'intolerable noise'. However, the specific cause of the noise has included building works in the house [6], dogs barking [7], music and fireworks [8], loud singing [9], gunfire [10], horses [11], children playing noisily at night [12], or crowing cockerels [13]. There is no closed list. The question to be addressed is whether there is a nuisance from the viewpoint of the victim of the noise [14].

[1] The common law test of nuisance is the same as that to be used in statutory nuisance proceedings: *Meri Mate v City of Dundee District Council,* 1994 SCLR (N) 960.

[2] There is, however, no absolute decibel level at which a noise becomes a nuisance. On measurement of noise levels and standards, see *British Standard 4142*. On the use of decibel levels in determination of nuisance see, *R v Fenny Stratford Justices, ex parte Watney Mann (Midlands) Ltd* [1976] 1 WLR 1101 and *East Northamptonshire District Council v Brian Fossett* [1994] Env LR 388.

[3] Noise includes vibration (Control of Pollution Act 1974, section 73(1)) and has been described as 'sound which is undesired by the recipient'. This simple description emphasises the cardinal fact that 'noise is subjective; a noise problem must involve people and their feelings, and its assessment is a matter of human values and environments rather than of precise physical measurement ... It is true that for many noises annoyance increases with loudness; but the annoying effects of a number of noises, all equally loud, will depend much more on the personality of the recipient than the character of the noise. It seems inconceivable that an "annoyance meter" should ever be designed which would be of practical use to the legislator, or that any universal scale of measurement could be introduced, other than that of normal common sense and consideration for others, by which the pleasure of a minority in some noisy pursuit could be balanced against the pain of a quieter majority.': *Report of the Wilson Committee on the Problem of Noise,* Cmnd. 2056 (1963), paragraphs 6, 35. For a recent and comprehensive treatment of the subject of noise, see Penn, *Noise Control: the law and its enforcement* (Shaw and Sons 1995).

[4] *Fergusson v McCulloch* 1953 SLT (Sh Ct) 113.

[5] 1873 8 Ch 467 at 471 *per* Mellish LJ. In such circumstances the question also arises as to whether the house or houses are adequately insulated. On the requirements for sound insulation in new buildings, see Building Standards (Scotland) Regulations 1990, SI 1990/2179, regulations 19–21; Hamilton et al (1993). *The Scottish Building Regulations Illustrated and Explained* (Blackwell). In summary, the 1990 Regulations require that walls, floors and stairs 'shall provide adequate resistance to the transmission' of airborne (e.g. speech, music etc.) and impact (e.g. footsteps) sound. On measurement of sound insulation in building elements, see BS 2750 (1980), parts 3 and 6; BS 5821 (1984), parts 1 and 2.

[6] *Andreae v Selfridge and Co Ltd* [1938] Ch 1.

[7] *Shanlin v Collins* 1973 SLT (Sh Ct) 21.

[8] *Walker v Brewster* (1867) LR 5 Eq 25. See also *Hampstead and Suburban Properties Ltd v Diomedous* [1968] 3 All ER 545 where it was held that it was necessary to consider 'whether it is more important for the plaintiff's tenants to have the relative peace and quiet in their homes to which they have been accustomed, or for the defendant's customers to have the pleasure of music while they eat, played at high volume. When this comparison is made, it seems to me that it is the home rather than the meal table which must prevail. A home in which sleep is possible is a necessity, whereas loud music as an accompaniment is, for those who enjoy it, relatively a luxury...'.

[9] *Motion v Mills* (1897) 13 TLR 427. "... Just conceive a *tenore robusto* endeavouring to teach his pupil to sing such a familiar song as "Sound an Alarm" and to reach the well known high note. Whether classical music was more distracting than works of a lower class [I] could not say...'.

[10] *Hollywood Silver Fox Farm v Emmett* [1936] 2 KB 468.

[11] *Ball v Ray,* supra.

[12] *Dunton v Dover District Council* (1978) 76 LGR 87, QBD.

[13] *Leeman v Montagu* [1936] 2 All ER 1677. Mr Montagu's neighbours claimed to have to sleep with cotton wool in their ears and likened the noise of the birds to a football crowd cheering a cup tie.

[14] *Watt v Jamieson* 1954 SC 56, approved in *Shanlin v Collins*, supra, at page 23.

4.5.4 Animals and Common Law Nuisance

To use an animal as a means of attacking or threatening another person or his/her property is (apart from any criminal liability which may also arise), a wrong actionable by interdict [1]. Examples include setting a dog to bite a neighbour [2] or riding a horse across someone's land with a view to causing damage [3]. The issues of noise, smell and faeces of animals go to the question of whether a common law nuisance is being causcd. Examples considered in the case law include the keeping of chickens [4] and barking dogs [5].

[1] Civil liability is also imposed on the owner of the animal for any damage caused to person or property: Animals (Scotland) Act 1987, section 1.

[2] *Camerons v Miller* (1908) 23 Sh Ct Reps 318.

[3] *Inverurie Mags v Sorrie* 1956 SLT(N) 17, 1956 SC 175.

[4] *Ireland v Smith* (1895) 3 SLT 180.

[5] *Spider's Web v Merchant* [1961] CLY 6359; *Shanlin v Collins* 1973 SLT (Sh Ct) 21.

4.5.5 Breach of Lease

The lease between landlord and tenant is a contract which creates mutual rights and obligations. If the tenant by his actions breaches or proposes to breach the lease his behaviour may be an actionable wrong and the subject of interdict [1]. In *Basildon District Council v Tugwell* [2], for example, an injunction [3] was brought against a tenant from keeping 18 dogs in breach of his lease thereby causing nuisance and annoyance to neighbours. Where the lease contains an express 'nuisance' prohibition, it does not matter that the particular behaviour in question may not constitute a nuisance at common law [4].

[1] Gloag on *Contract* (2nd edition, 1929), page 602, Walker, *Civil Remedies*, page 233.

[2] (unrep.) 7th July 1993, Brentwood County Court, LAG, March 1995, page 11. The provision in the lease apparently read that the tenant was to 'ensure at all times that any pets kept on the premises do not by their behaviour cause any nuisance, annoyance or inconvenience'.

[3] The English equivalent of interdict.

[4] Bells *Principles*, s. 974; *Manson v Forrest* (1887) 14 R 802.

4.5.6 It is essential that the lease clearly specifies the conduct which is sought to be prohibited [1]. In *London Borough of Lewisham v Simba-Tola* [2], an interlocutory injunction was sought against an anti-social tenant on the basis of the nuisance clause in the lease. It was held that the covenants in the lease were 'not apt to comprehend the conduct of which complaint was made'. As there was no common law basis on which the injunction could alternatively be based, the order was refused [3]. Accordingly, if landlords wish to use interdict to deal with tenant conduct cases they should examine their leases, and ensure that they contain adequate provision in respect of nuisance and annoyance clauses [4].

[1] *Lawson v Hay* 1989 GWD 24-1049.

[2] (1991) 24 HLR 644.

[3] The lease provided that 'the tenant must not do anything on or around the dwelling or on the estate of which the dwelling forms a part or on or around any other housing property of the council, which in the opinion of the council is or may become a nuisance, annoyance or cause offence to other people'. The conduct against which the order was sought related, however, to the tenant's conduct at and around the council's offices.

[4] Particularly in the light of *Dundee District Council v Cook* 1995 SCLR (N) 559, paragraph 4.3 above. Landlords may vary leases by agreement with the tenants or by using the powers in section 54 of the Housing (Scotland) Act 1987 (secure tenancies) or section 17 of the Housing (Scotland) Act 1988 (statutory assured tenancies).

4.5.7 Breach of Feudal Conditions

Breach of feudal conditions may give rise to a right of interdict [1]. This may be considered where the perpetrator of the neighbour nuisance is not a tenant, but an owner-occupier. The 'owner' of any house in Scotland holds it in law on the basis of such feudal conditions as may be contained in the title deeds. While these may not deal with the behaviour of the owner *per se*, they often set down prohibitions on use of the house, typically that it should not be used to run any business, or that certain building works on the land can only be undertaken with the consent of the feudal superior. The local authority selling a house to a former tenant under the right to buy legislation has the power to impose reasonable conditions in the title: these might include prohibitions against certain kinds of neighbour nuisance [2]. If the owner of the house were to breach such a condition, then interdict may be sought [3]. The title conditions may also create a right in a third party to bring interdict proceedings [4].

[1] This is a complex subject which is outwith the scope of this work. For more information, see textbooks on conveyancing: for example, Halliday, *Conveyancing Law and Practice* (4 volumes) (1985); MacDonald, *Conveyancing Manual* (4th edition, 1994).

[2] Housing (Scotland) Act 1987, section 64(1). This is frequently done in practice.

[3] *Lawson v Hay,* supra.

[4] The *jus quaesitum tertio:* see *Lees v North East Fife District Council* 1987 SC 265, 1987 SLT 769. Conditions inserted in the offer of sale of a council house may be for the benefit of neighbours: *Coull v City of Aberdeen District Council* (unrep.) Lands Tribunal, 10th March 1982 noted in P.Q. Watchman (1991), *Housing (Scotland) Act 1987* (annotated), Greens, page 152.

4.6 Having ascertained that the act which is complained of is in fact wrongful, there must be reasonable apprehension that it will occur in the future or continue to occur if already started [1]. This may of course be inferred from past behaviour, but just because a tenant has had one noisy party, this does not necessarily give reasonable cause to believe that they will have another, although all the circumstances of the individual case have to be considered. If, on the other hand, the wrong is a continuing one, such as running a car repair business from the front yard, then this in itself may suggest that the wrong will continue to occur in the future. Prior to raising any action, however, there should be a call on the tenant not to do the wrong which is anticipated, or continuing, or the interdict action might fall to be dismissed [2].

[1] *Hays Trs v Young* (1877) 4 R 398.

[2] *Hays Trs v Young,* supra; *Caledonian Railway v Glasgow Magistrates* (1897) 25 R 74.

4.7 Positive and Negative Interdicts

It is not permissible to interdict a person in order to force them to do a positive act, but only to *prevent* them from doing something: otherwise the correct court action is one for specific implement [1]. The problem arises where a pursuer tries to disguise a positive order in the form of a double negative [2]. For example, a landlord could interdict a tenant not to dump noxious waste in his garden, but not to require him (by means of interdict) to remove waste already dumped there. Nor could he get around this problem by seeking to interdict him against continuing to have the waste in his garden which was already there [3].

[1] *Wemyss v Ardrossan Harbour Co* (1893) 20 R 500.

[2] Burn Murdoch, *Interdict,* paragraph 168/9. The matter is conceptually complex: see 'Positive and Negative Interdicts', 1990 JLS 453 and 510; Scott Robinson, *Law of Interdict* (1994), pages 3-4.

[3] For a recent example of how this problem may manifest itself when trying to interdict against breach of lease, see *Church Commissioners for England v Abbey National plc* 1994 SLT 959, 1994 SCLR 867. The landlord may, however, seek an order for specific implement, i.e. an order obliging the tenant to do some positive act in fulfilment of his legal duties. This has its own problems, particularly in relation to specification of the crave. See e.g. *Postel Properties Ltd v Miller and Santhouse plc* 1993 SLT 353, 1992 SCLR 799; *Retail Parks Investments Ltd v Royal Bank of Scotland* 1996 SLT 669; Walker: Civil Remedies chapter 13. Note also, however, that the Court of Session has wide powers to grant interim orders including interim implement: Court of Session Act 1988, section 47. In very serious cases the landlord might consider raising proceedings in the Court of Session, if, say, in the previous example the noxious waste was thought to include asbestos.

4.8 Interdict Procedure in the Sheriff Court

4.8.1 The jurisdiction of the sheriff court to hear a case is based on the defender's domicile or the place where it is anticipated that the wrong will be committed [1]. The landlord's solicitor drafts and lodges an initial writ [2] detailing the landlord's title and interest, the anti-social conduct complained of, any relevant terms of the lease and how the conduct constitutes an actionable wrong. The writ should also narrate in detail the efforts already made short of court action to persuade the tenant to behave, and why it is reasonably to be apprehended that the wrong will occur or continue. The crave of the writ narrates the order which the landlord is asking the court to make. This must be framed with care and precision, enabling the defender to know precisely those acts which henceforth s/he is to be prohibited from doing [3]. As an interdict is a personal order, only those individuals (correctly) named as defenders will be subject to the order for interdict if granted [4]. The writ should also crave interim interdict. Interim interdict is 'a discretionary remedy granted to regulate, and where possible preserve, the right of parties, pending the final determination of the matter in issue' [5].

[1] Civil Jurisdiction and Judgments Act 1982, Schedule 8, paragraph 2. Interdict is also competent in the Court of Session.

[2] Ordinary Cause Rules 1993, rule 3.1 and Form G1.

[3] *Webster v Lord Advocate* 1985 SC 173, 1985 SLT 361; *Kelso School Board v Hunter* (1874) 2 R 228 at 232 *per* Lord Deas; Walker, *Civil Remedies,* page 223; *Griffiths and Griffiths v MacIntyre and MacIntyre* (unrep.) 9th July 1986, Hamilton Sheriff Court, Sheriff Principal Gillies.

[4] *Shell Ltd, Petrs,* 1995 GWD 25-1353.

[5] Scott Robinson, *Law of Interdict,* page 173.

4.8.2   On lodging the writ with the court, the landlord's solicitor seeks an immediate hearing (usually within 24 hours) before the sheriff, at which point a motion can be made for an interim interdict to be granted, and for warrant to serve the writ on the defender. A second hearing may also be fixed at this time (usually about seven days later). This practice varies from sheriffdom to sheriffdom. At the first hearing, when the defender is not present [1], the landlord's solicitor will narrate the terms of the writ to the sheriff, and give any additional ex parte evidence requested. The tests for the sheriff at this stage are whether (i) there is prima facie a case to try (including whether the landlord has title and interest to sue) and (ii) whether the 'balance of convenience' favours the grant of the order [2]. The sheriff may grant or refuse interim interdict at his or her discretion, or only grant interdict after amendment of the crave.

[1] Except in the unlikely event that s/he has previously lodged a caveat – see MacPhail, *Sheriff Court Practice,* paragraph 21.75.

[2] *Deane v Lothian Regional Council* 1986 SLT 22; *Nicol v Blott* 1986 SLT 677.

4.8.3   Factors which may affect the decision whether to grant interim interdict are whether there is danger to the public [1] or 'manifest injuria' – an 'apprehension of personal injury, or of danger to life or of great and perhaps irreparable loss' [2]. It is irrelevant for the purposes of the court proceedings that there may be little prospect that the defender will comply with the terms of the interdict, or that it might not be 'reasonable' with regard to the personal hardship of the defender [3]. If the interim interdict is granted, a copy of the initial writ and the court order granting the interim interdict (together with notice of the date of any second hearing) must be immediately and personally served on the tenant, usually by sheriff officer. Immediately service has been effected, the tenant is bound by order of the court to desist from the interdicted behaviour.

[1]   In *Cumbernauld Development Corporation v Marsh* 1990 GWD 38-2221, 1991 GWD 34 2092, interdict was obtained against a tenant of a mobile home from using bottled gas fuel on the basis of the danger to neighbouring residents.

[2]   Burn Murdoch, *Interdict; Singer v Kimball & Morton* (1873) 11 M 267.

[3]   *Sutton Housing Trust v Lawrence* (1987) 19 HLR 520.

4.8.4   Where a second hearing has been fixed the defender will have an opportunity to appear or be represented and to show cause why the order for interim interdict should not be continued. If s/he does not appear, the interim interdict will normally be continued by the sheriff without further ado. If the tenant or tenant's solicitor appears and opposes the continuation of the interdict, the sheriff must again address the question of where the balance of convenience lies. The sheriff may hear ex parte evidence from the defender's solicitor or direct evidence from the defender if present, but will not adjudicate at this stage as to conflicts on the facts, nor overly scrutinise the written pleadings [1]. If, therefore, the landlord has averred a material breach of the lease, and the tenant cannot show that s/he would be prejudiced by the interdict, then it is likely that the balance of convenience will favour the landlord, even if the tenant denies the behaviour. A key question often is 'would the tenant be prevented by this interim interdict from doing something which he would not lawfully be able to do anyway?' In other words, even if the tenant denies having loud parties every night, if s/he is not permitted to do so by the terms of the lease, then s/he cannot be prejudiced by the interim interdict. Alternatively, the defender may avoid the grant or continuation of interim interdict by giving an undertaking to the court that s/he will cease or not carry out the wrongful conduct [2].

[1] *Scottish Universal Newspapers v Smith* 1982 SLT 160; *Group 4 Total Security v Ferrier* 1985 SC 70, 1985 SLT 287.

[2] *Grant & Sons v Cadenhead* 1985 SC 121, 1985 SLT 291.

4.8.5   In the great majority of cases, therefore, if serious anti-social behaviour has been alleged, and the writ is competently drafted, interim interdict will be granted. Even if refused at the first hearing, or recalled at the second, the landlord may still continue with the action seeking permanent interdict without the protection of an interim interdict, bearing in mind that if a further incident occurs a fresh motion for interim interdict may be made. In practice, many defenders will simply not turn up for a second hearing. Whether s/he does or does not appear, if the interim interdict is not recalled, s/he may choose not to defend the action any further. In this case the landlord may simply minute for decree for permanent interdict, normally after 21 days from the date of service. If the tenant does choose to defend the action and seeks to prevent the grant of a permanent interdict, s/he will require to lodge written answers to the initial writ within 21 days of service, and the case will proceed as a normal ordinary cause action. This may take many months if vigorously defended, but without a further order of the court, any interim interdict granted will continue in force until either permanent interdict is granted or the case is successfully defended.

4.9   Breach of Interdict

4.9.1   The person complaining of a breach of interdict [1] must start a new court action for breach of interdict with a new initial writ. The 'consent and concurrence' of the procurator fiscal to the action proceeding must be sought, as the facts narrated may give grounds for criminal prosecution [2]. The new writ will narrate the terms of the interdict in force, and details of the fresh behaviour allegedly in breach of it. This is served on the defender, who is ordained to appear personally before the sheriff. Failure to appear when summoned may lead to a warrant being issued for the defender's arrest, or a fine being imposed in absence [3]. If the defender denies the alleged breach, the matter will proceed to a hearing at which the parties will lead evidence to attempt to establish or refute that the breach has occurred [4]. If found guilty of the breach of interdict the sheriff has a wide range of punishments. A breach of interdict is 'a challenge to the authority of the court and punishable by admonition, censure, fine or imprisonment' [5]. It is no defence to a breach of interdict action to claim that the interdict itself was wrongly granted [6]. For guidelines as to the appropriateness or otherwise of imprisonment for breach of interdict, see *Forbes v Forbes* [7].

[1] Including interim interdict: it is not open to the defender in a breach of interdict action to argue that the interdict itself should not have been granted. In practice, from the point of view of a landlord most difficulties are encountered not in obtaining interdicts (and interim interdicts) but in responding to a breach of the interdict.

[2] In practice this would appear to be something of a formality. *Gribben v Gribben* 1976 SLT 266; MacPhail, *Sheriff Court Practice*, paragraph 21.85.

[3] *Anderson v Connacher* (1850) 13 D 405. This should have particular resonance for tenant defenders of eviction actions where non-attendance at court is frequent. In breach of interdict proceedings, the tenant cannot, except at his peril, escape having to answer personally to the court for his actions.

[4] Procedural matters in relation to actions for breach of interdict were considered in the case of *Griffiths and Griffiths v MacIntyre and MacIntyre*, supra, paragraph 4.8.1. If the defender denies the breach, it is desirable that written answers be lodged on his behalf and that evidence at the proof is recorded by shorthand writer. The interlocutor granting the original interdict must be obtained and lodged in process. Its terms must be specific and properly tied into the crave. It is the pursuer's responsibility to ensure that it is so. Its terms must be incorporated expressly or by reference into the pleadings in the breach of interdict action. The standard of proof at this hearing is the criminal (beyond reasonable doubt) rather than the civil standard (balance of probabilities) see *Eutectic Welding Alloys v Whitting* 1969 SLT(Notes) 79. However, the proceedings are civil (only) for the purposes of section 1(1) of the Civil Evidence (Scotland) Act 1988, and accordingly no corroboration is required.

[5] *Johnson v Grant* 1923 SC 789; Scott Robinson, Chapter 16.

[6] *Dick v Fleshers of Stirling* (1827) 5 S 268.

[7] 1994 SLT 16, 1993 SCLR 348. In particular, the questions asked by the Extra Division in this case were those of (a) the affront to the administration of justice (b) whether the actings by the person in the breach have been to the detriment of the other party and (c) whether the defender has apologised for the breach and taken steps to mitigate its effects. The court also referred to the dicta in *McIntyre v Sheridan* (unrep.) 26th March 1992, Inner House, where the Lord Ordinary was said to be 'well founded in concluding that there had been a flagrant and calculated breach of interim interdict ... [and that] ... civil imprisonment was well nigh inevitable.'

4.9.2 The landlord is not obliged to pursue a breach of interdict action. It remains possible to seek eviction by proceeding with an action for recovery of possession. The statement of claim in such an action could narrate that an interdict against the behaviour had been obtained but that the behaviour had continued. This will demonstrate to the court that the landlord had countenanced other legal methods of controlling the tenant's behaviour but that these had been unsuccessful. It will also demonstrate that the tenant had full knowledge of the conduct complained of. Finally, the question of whether the tenant has misbehaved can be considered on the basis of the 'balance of probabilities', rather than 'beyond reasonable doubt'. The sheriff will not, in the context of the repossession action, have the quasi-criminal powers to dispose of the case that he has in a breach of interdict action, but if the sheriff is satisfied that the misbehaviour has occurred despite the existence of an interdict, this may indicate to him/her that the tenant has disregarded the authority of the court. This may be material in assessment of the question of reasonableness in the repossession action.

4.9.3 There is similarly nothing to stop the landlord raising interdict proceedings at the same time as an action for possession [1]. If interim interdict is obtained, and the tenant's behaviour does not improve, then the landlord has lost nothing by using interdict proceedings, but can bring the possession action to a conclusion as swiftly as possible. If the tenant's behaviour improves, however, then the repossession action can be sisted (i.e. suspended). If conditions subsequently deteriorate again, the landlord can prevent any delay in proceeding with eviction, as the sisted action can simply be revived and a proof fixed [2].

[1] See, for example, in England: *Basildon District Council v Mills* (unrep.) 27th September 1994, Brentwood County Court, LAG, March 1995, page 11; *London Borough of Lewisham v Simba-Tola* (1991) 24 HLR 644.

[2] This would be to hold something of a 'Sword of Damocles' over the tenant's head. On the other hand, if the tenant's behaviour had improved over a lengthy period of time, then it would be open to him or her to move for recall of the sist, and to seek dismissal of the action. Even if the facts were admitted, it could be argued that because of the passage of time and the tenants improved behaviour it would now be unreasonable to evict.

4.10 Edinburgh District Council has been the subject of the first Scottish study of the use of interdict as a remedy in relation to neighbour nuisance [1]. Over a period from December 1993 to November 1994, this authority brought 15 actions of interdict. Of these, only one was successfully defended at the stage of interim interdict [2]. In all but three of these cases eviction action was also initiated, either at the same time as the interdict action or subsequently. At the date of writing of the study, five of the tenants had in fact been evicted (one for rent arrears). In five of the cases the outcome included the finding that the behaviour giving rise to the complaints had stopped. The study notes that the introduction of the policy came against resistance from legal staff and was as a result of 'political' pressure due to the need to be seen to be 'doing something' about neighbour nuisance. This reluctance and scepticism about the process is thought to have coloured its use. Staff continue to see eviction as the main legal weapon. Interdict and breach of interdict are seen as 'too complex' by legal staff. The study concludes that interdicts can be effective in some neighbour nuisance situations, but are far from a legal panacea. In particular, more guidance, training and monitoring of the policy is said to be required.

[1] C. Scott (1995) *'Landlord Interdicts: the experience of Edinburgh District Council'* Housing Diploma Research Paper, University of Stirling.

[2] The policy of this council is apparently never to progress the interdict action beyond interim orders. If the tenant does acts in breach of the interdict, eviction action is initiated. The bringing of breach of interdict actions is thought to be 'a long drawn out process as yet untested ... eviction action is the quicker and more final solution favoured by legal staff'.

5 LAWBURROWS

Lawburrows is an ancient Scottish remedy against anticipated physical harm to a person or damage to property. Although seldom used, it has some advantages over other remedies in some neighbour nuisance situations.

5.1 In an application to the court for lawburrows [1], it is alleged that there is a risk of harm to the complainer, his family or property from another person – for example, a neighbour. The objective is to prevent 'delinquencies': a more powerful alternative to reparation after the event [2]. The remedy dates from the Lawburrows Acts of 1429 and 1581, with the procedure now regulated by the Civil Imprisonment (Scotland) Act 1882, section 6. Except as expressly modified by the 1882 Act, the older principles still apply. The application to the court is for an order requiring the respondent to find caution (or to grant a bond of caution) [3] for a sum of money to be determined by the court, failing which imprisonment for a fixed period or until caution is found. If the respondent contravenes lawburrows, the applicant may raise a further action for contravention. If successful, the caution will be forfeit. Although infrequently used [4], lawburrows has certain advantages over other remedies which are considered below.

[1] Lawburrows derives from the word 'borrow' or 'borgh' (borh) meaning caution (pronounced 'kayshun'). Caution is a deposit of money with the court which is forfeit if the order of the court is broken. More detailed treatments of the subject can be found in Walker, *Civil Remedies* (Greens 1974), and *Stair Memorial Encyclopaedia,* vol. 10.

[2] Stair, *Institutes,* I.ix.30.

[3] I.e. a guarantee that the amount of caution will be made available in the event that the court determines that caution shall be forfeit.

[4] In particular, see *Morrow v Neil* 1975 SLT (Sh Ct) 65 – a judgment of Sheriff MacPhail which contains a detailed exposition of the substance and procedure of the law. See also *Porteus v Rutherford* 1980 SLT (Sh Ct) 129; *Mackenzie v Maclennan* 1916 SC 617; *MacLeod v MacLeod* 1928 SLT (Sh Ct) 27.

5.2 To obtain an order for lawburrows, the applicant must show that he has reasonable cause to believe that the respondent will cause bodily harm to him, his family or property [1]. The harm may be of any kind [2]. 'Reasonable cause' has been shown, for example, by receipt of threatening letters [3], previous damage to property coupled with a background of threats and abuse [4], and testimony of witnesses to verbal threats [5].

However, lawburrows is not concerned with remedying dislike between neighbours or bad manners [6], nor thoughtless inconvenience [7]. Lawburrows may be sought against anyone except a child [8]. It may be sought against corporate bodies [9]. Lawburrows may have application in the context of serious neighbour nuisance (i.e. actual or threatened violence or damage), rather than lesser nuisances (e.g. noise or immoral behaviour).

[1] *Morrow v Neil,* supra at 67; *Brock v Rankine* (1874) 1 R 991 at 1002. Lawburrows cannot be sought by a landlord unless its own property is at risk since it would not have title and interest to sue. See para 4.3 above.

[2] Walker *Civil Remedies* (Greens 1974), page 1210 (including defamation).

[3] *Brock v Rankine,* supra.

[4] *Morton and Morton v Liddle* (unrep.) 29th May 1995, Perth Sheriff Court (Case No. B1094/992). In this colourful case the defender was found to have been responsible for smashing the pursuer's window, throwing a log through his glass front door, and damaging a fence thereby allowing sheep to escape. The more lurid incidents included writing the letters 'R.I.P'. in a patch of newly laid concrete, placing a condom over the bolt of a gate, and suspending a full-size cardboard skeleton in full view of the pursuer's house, complete with a luminous penis and a message describing him as 'the biggest dick in town'. After granting lawburrows, the sheriff noted that the defender's evidence was plainly 'distorted by an overwhelming sense of injustice' although the roots of this 'remained obscure even after proof'. The Defender's appeal was dismissed 1996 GWD 24-1298.

[5] Stair, *Institutes,* IV.xlviii. 15.

[6] *Morrow v Neil,* supra.

[7] *Porteous v Rutherford,* supra (noisy parties).

[8] *Seytoun v Ballingall* (1532) Mor. 8023. Age of Legal Capacity (Scotland) Act 1991, section 1(3)(f).

[9] *Reid v Sheriffdom of Ayr* (1541) Mor. 8023; *Old Town of Aberdeen v New Town* (1549) Mor. 8026.

5.3 The burden of proof is on the applicant, on the civil standard [1]. This is despite the fact that the procedure at proof is governed by the Summary Jurisdiction Acts [2]. Corroboration is not required [3].

[1] I.e. proof on the balance of probabilities: *Morrow v Neil,* supra at 69.

[2] 1882 Act, section 6(3); *Morrow v Neil,* supra at 69

[3] 1882 Act, section 6(4); Civil Evidence (Scotland) Act 1988, section 1. If corroborative evidence is available, it should of course be led.

5.4 Procedure under the 1882 Act is intended to be swift: accordingly there are no written defences, preliminary pleas, debates or continuations [1]. The action is commenced by summary application or initial writ [2]. The application should crave the court to order the respondent to find caution of lawburrows (or a bond of caution) for a specified amount against harm to the applicant, his family and property, failing which imprisonment for a specific period [3]. The application should also seek warrant to cite witnesses and expenses [4]. The application should aver the factual circumstances supporting the application. The application is then presented to the court. On warrant being granted, the court should immediately fix a proof [5]. At the diet of proof, the action must be disposed of summarily [6]. Appeal against the sheriff's judgment is by way of stated case [7].

[1] *Morrow v Neil,* supra.

[2] Both forms of application have been used in modern times: *Morrow v Neil,* supra (initial writ); *Morton and Morton v Liddle,* supra (summary application).

[3] The amount of caution is in the discretion of the court: 1882 Act, section 6(5). The maximum period of imprisonment is six months by a sheriff or sheriff principal; 14 days by a justice of the peace: 1882 Act, section 6(6). See *Morton and Morton v Liddle,* supra (order for £500.00 or 4 weeks imprisonment); *Porteus v Rutherford,* supra (£250.00 or six months).

[4] For style craves see *Morrow v Neil,* supra at 66; *Porteous v Rutherford,* supra at 129.

[5] 1882 Act, section 6(2). The practice may be, however, to ignore this very summary procedure: see *Morrow v Neil,* supra at 70.

[6] 1882 Act, section 6(3): i.e. no defences need be lodged.

[7] Under the Summary Jurisdiction (Scotland) Act 1954: *Mackenzie v Maclennan,* supra.

5.5 Where the pursuer establishes his/her case, the application is granted by the court. Nothing further will happen unless the pursuer alleges that further wrongful acts have occurred. Enforcing a contravention of lawburrows requires a separate action [1]. The burden of proof is on the applicant, probably to the criminal standard [2]. If the contravention is proved, the court may order the caution to be forfeit [3]. It appears that the caution is divided equally between the applicant and the Crown [4]. The court should imprison for the fixed period where the caution is not paid over [5].

[1] Walker, *Civil Remedies,* page 1211.

[2] I.e. beyond reasonable doubt, as the action is penal in nature: Erskine, *Institutes,* IV.i.16; *Morrow v Neil,* supra at 69.

[3] Or payment recovered from the cautioner, if a bond of caution was originally given.

[4] Lawburrows Act 1581.

[5] I.e. the court has no discretion: *Morrow v Neil*, supra at 67.

5.6 Lawburrows has been rarely used in modern times. Interdict seems to be used in preference, and it will be apparent that the two remedies are similar. In *Morrow v Neil*, Sheriff MacPhail suggested the following advantages to using lawburrows in an appropriate case:

- In interdict actions, the court has a discretion to refuse interdict in the public interest even if the grounds for interdict are established. No such discretion is available in lawburrows.

- Interdict merely ordains the defender to refrain from a course of action. Lawburrows also orders the defender to take the active step of lodging money, or a bond, on pain of imprisonment.

- If an interdict is breached, the consequences for the defender are uncertain for both parties as the court has discretion as to penalty. In lawburrows, the penalty is preordained and therefore known in advance.

- The court procedure for lawburrows (if correctly followed) may be simpler, speedier and less expensive than interdict.

5.7 On the other hand, there are disadvantages to the use of lawburrows as against interdict:

- There is no order analogous to interim interdict in an action for lawburrows.

- The applicant must prove threatened or actual physical harm to body or property: threatened nuisance or annoyance is insufficient.

6 STATUTORY NUISANCE

Local authorities have powers and duties under statute to prevent or abate prescribed events or conduct which cause nuisance or are 'prejudicial to health'. Some of these powers and duties are relevant to anti-social behaviour and may provide effective remedies.

6.1 Introduction

Some neighbour nuisance may constitute a statutory nuisance under environmental and related legislation [1]. If so, the local authority has the power, and indeed the duty, to take action [2]. There is a considerable quantity of literature available on the subject [3]. Those provisions of the legislation relevant to anti-social behaviour are now examined.

[1] The relevant legislation is the Environmental Protection Act 1990 (Part III) brought into force in Scotland on 1 April 1996 by section 107 of the Environment Act 1995: Environmental Protection Act (Commencement Order No. 5) Order 1996, SI 1996/186. On this date, those provisions of the Public Health (Scotland) Act 1897 and the Control of Pollution Act 1974 dealing with statutory nuisance (including noise pollution) were repealed by the 1995 Act (See Schedule 24). Scots law thus was brought into line with English law. Sections 81A and 81B of the 1990 Act (relating to placing of charges on property for sums due to local authorities) will not, however, extend to Scotland. Nor will the Scottish court have any power to impose fines on making of an abatement order : 1990 Act, Section 82(2). The Noise and Statutory Nuisance Act 1993, (which amended Part II of the 1990 Act in part) also applies to Scotland and makes provision for regulation of loudspeakers in roads (Schedule 2) and burglar alarms (section 9 and Schedule 3). Section 9 and Schedule 3 are not yet in force. Cases decided under the now repealed parts of the 1974 and 1897 Acts may still be of value in interpreting Part III of the 1990 as many of the provisions are similar if not identical. English cases decided under the 1990 Act will, of course, be highly relevant now.

[2] See 1990 Act, Section 79(1), Section 80.

[3] See for example: Tromans, Nash and Poustie (1996) The Environmental Acts 1990 – 1995, 3rd ed. Sweet and Maxwell; Stair Memorial Encyclopaedia, volume 9; (Both of these works have been of considerable assistance in preparing this chapter); Stair Memorial Encyclopaedia, Environment, Volume 9, Public Health, Volume 19; The Encyclopaedia of Environmental Law, (six volumes), Sweet and Maxwell. For a short narration of the relevant provisions of the 1990 Act, see Dunkley and Murdie, Statutory Nuisance, LAG, February 1995, p19.

6.2 Environmental Protection Act 1990

6.2.1 Statutory Nuisance

Section 79 defines "statutory nuisances" which are regulated by Part III of the Act. A statutory nuisance occurs [1] if one of several prescribed events exists which is "a nuisance or prejudicial to health" [2]. Where a statutory nuisance exists, a local authority is under a duty to take action and an individual has the power to initiate legal proceedings. These matters are considered further below [3]. Certain statutory nuisances are analysed in more detail first however.

[1] The 1990 Act was amended by The Noise and Statutory Nuisance Act 1993: see para 6.3 *infra*. Those relevant to neighbour nuisance are as follows: (a) any premises in such a state as to be prejudicial to health or a nuisance; (b) smoke emitted from premises so as to be prejudicial to health or a nuisance (not smoke from a chimney or a private dwelling in a smoke control area: s79(3)); (c) fumes or gases emitted from premises so as to be prejudicial to health or a nuisance (private dwellings only: s79(4)); (d) any accumulation or deposit which is prejudicial to health or a nuisance; (e) any animal kept in such a manner or place as to be prejudicial to health or a nuisance; (f) noise emitted from a premises so as to be prejudicial to health or a nuisance; (g) noise that is prejudicial to health or a nuisance and is emitted from or caused by a vehicle, machinery or equipment in a road; (g) any other matter declared by any enactment to be a statutory nuisance.

[2] Nuisance is not further defined in the Act – it is the common law definition which is relevant (see paragraph 4.5.1. *et. seq. supra*) as well as circumstances prejudicial to health. See *Meri-Mate v Dundee District Council* 1994 SCLR (N) 960 and cases cited therein. The English common law of nuisance is not identical to the Scots law position, so caution must be exercised in considering English cases relating to the definition of nuisance. Prejudicial to health" is defined by section 79(7) as meaning "injurious, or likely to cause injury to health". This definition of statutory nuisance corresponds broadly with that contained within section 16(1) of the Public Health (Scotland) Act 1897 ("nuisance or injurious or dangerous to health"). If a nuisance, it may not necessary to show also that it is also prejudicial to health – see paragraph 6.2.1.1. n.3. *infra*. To prove prejudice to health, it would normally be essential to lead expert evidence supporting the contention that the circumstances are, or would be, prejudicial to health. Such experts could include medical general practitioners, medical consultants, appropriate officers from official bodies such as the local authority environmental health department or Health and Safety Executive, university academics from an appropriate discipline.

[3] At paragraphs 6.2.2 *et. seq.*

6.2.1.1 Premises

Any premises in such a state as to be prejudicial to health or a nuisance is a statutory nuisance [1]. "Premises" includes land and any vessel [2]. It may not be necessary to show that the premises are prejudicial to health if they are in such a state as to be a nuisance [3]. Premises which are inadequately insulated against noise may fall into this category [4].

[1] 1990 Act, section 79(1)(a)

[2] 1990 Act, section 79(7), except steam powered reciprocating machinery.

[3] For cases decided under the now repealed provisions of the 1897 Act, see *Renfrew District Council v McGourlick* 1988 SLT 127, 1987 SLT 538; *McGeechan and Others v Inverclyde District Council* (unrep.) 3 October 1985; Greenock Sheriff Court, Sheriff Smith. In *Betts v Penge Urban District Council* (1942) 2 KB 154, it was held sufficient to show interference with personal comfort (removal of front door and window sashes constituted statutory nuisance). However, other cases have held that the nuisance part is to be qualified by reference to the general spirit of the Public Health Acts; which are concerned with health and disease matters. See for example *Coventry City Council v Cartwright* [1975] 1 WLR 845 (deposit of materials) and *National Coal Board v Neath Borough Council* [1976] 2 All ER 478 at page 482 ("a nuisance cannot arise, if what has taken place affects only the person or persons occupying the premises where the nuisance is said to have taken place"). It remains to be seen whether cases referring to the "spirit of the Public Health Acts" will carry the same weight in the context of the interpretation of provisions now contained in a general environmental protection statute.

[4] See *Southwark London Borough Council v Ince* (1989) 21 HLR 504, where tenants of the Borough were successful in obtaining an order requiring the Borough to upgrade sound insulation against noise from a nearby road and railway. See also *Jacovides v Camden London Borough Council,* (unrep), 2 June 1994, Wells Street Magistrates Court and *Johnston v Hackney London Borough Council* (unrep*)* 30 March 1994, Wells St Magistrates Court, LAG August 1994, page 18. In *Rossell v London Borough of Southwark,* (unrep), *November 1985,* (cited in (1988) JPL 79), the local authority itself was the 'person responsible' for having undertaken conversions in blocks of flats which enabled everyday living sounds to cause nuisance in adjoining flats. See also *Network Housing Association Limited v Westminster City Council* [1995] Env. L.R. 176; (1995) 27 HLR 189; and an article by Bettle in 1988 J.P.L. 79. Simply removing the occupants may not be sufficient: see 6.2.2.5.n.2 *infra*. It is understood that certain Scottish local authorities, including Glasgow City Council have adopted this interpretation and are serving abatement notices on landlords requiring upgrading of sound insulation. See paragraph 4.5.3 n.5. regarding standards of sound insulation.

6.2.1.2 Deposits of Waste

Any accumulation or deposit which is prejudicial to health or a nuisance is a statutory nuisance [1]. This may be relevant to complaints of neighbours failing to use proper means of depositing household refuse, particularly perishable materials [2].

[1] 1990 Act, section 79(1)(e): similar to section 16(5) of the Public Health (Scotland) Act 1897. In *Coventry City Council v Cartwright* [1975] 1 WLR 845, it was held that the 'spirit' of the then English public health legislation was that it did not apply to a pile of building materials, scrap iron, broken glass and tin cans. Such debris was inert and could only cause injury to those coming onto the land and walking on the rubbish (as opposed to, say, rotting foodstuffs which could lead to rats and disease). Again, it remains to be seen if the new statutory vehicle for nuisance will alter judicial views.

[2] Particularly where the offender is not a tenant of the local authority. If s/he is, other remedies exist in addition: see paragraphs 4.4 *infra* and 10.1 *supra*. See also *City of Glasgow District Council v Walsh* (unrep.) 30 November 1984, Glasgow Sheriff Court (author of nuisance in relation to person providing harbourage for vermin under 1897 Act).

6.2.1.3 Animals

The keeping of animals is not a statutory nuisance as such [1]. However, any animal kept in such a place or manner as to be prejudicial to health or a nuisance, will constitute a statutory nuisance [2]. The wording of this definition is significantly different to earlier legislation and will encompass some situations not previously covered [3].

[1] Although it may be in breach of a tenancy agreement or deed of conditions (see paragraph 10.1 *infra*) or a criminal offence (see paragraph 3.3.10 *supra*). Where the animal is causing annoyance, any person can seek a control order (see paragraph 3.3.10.7 *supra*). See paragraph 4.5.4 *supra* regarding animals and common law nuisance.

[2] 1990 Act, Section 79(1)(f). See *Myatt v Teignbridge District Council* [1995] Env.L.R. 78 (17 dogs kept in small cottage causing nuisance to neighbours).

[3] Under section 16(4) of the Public Health (Scotland) Act 1897, the statutory nuisance was defined as "any stable, byre or other building in which any animal or animals are kept in such a manner or in such numbers as to be a nuisance or injurious to health". In *City of Glasgow District Council v Carroll* 1991 SLT (Sh. Ct.) 46, 1991 SCLR 199, the tenant was served with a notice relating to cats kept in her flat. It was held that there was no statutory nuisance as the flat was not a "stable, byre or other building" and secondly, because it was not the premises that was a nuisance but the urine impregnated soft furnishings within them. It is suggested that this case would not now be followed. See also *Morrisey v Galer* [1955] 1 WLR 110 where it was held that the noise resulting from keeping of greyhounds did not amount to a nuisance under the then English legislation, although nuisance might be caused by their smell. However, in *Coventry City Council v Cartwright (supra)* it was held that the wording was apt to cover noise.

6.2.1.4 Noise

Noise [1] emitted from premises so as to be prejudicial to health is a statutory nuisance [2]. A single event may be sufficient [3]. Noise that is prejudicial to health or a nuisance and is emitted from or caused by a vehicle, machinery, or equipment in a road, is also a statutory nuisance [4]. This is intended, in particular, to cover nuisance covered by unattended car alarms [5]. Special enforcement procedures apply to such noise [6].

[1] Noise includes vibration: 1990 Act, section 79(7). It excludes noise from aircraft other than model aircraft (s79(6)) and military premises (s79(2)).

[2] 1990 Act, section 79(1)(g). Noise nuisance was governed by Part III of the Control of Pollution Act 1974 prior to 1 April 1996. Premises includes land and any vessel : section 79(7). Thus, events such as raves and outdoor parties are covered as well as noise from within a house or flat etc. Noise caused by animals may alternatively be covered by section 79(1)(f): see paragraph 6.2.1.3 *supra*. See para 4.5.3 *supra* for commentary on noise nuisance at common law. See paragraph 3.3.8 *supra* regarding criminal offences and noise. 'Nuisance' should be given its common law meaning: *Meri Mate v City of Dundee District Council* 1994 SCLR (N) 960.

[3] That is, no repetition may be necessary: see *East Northamptonshire District Council v Fossett* [1994] Env. L. R. 388, a case relating to a proposed all night rave.

[4] 1990 Act, section 79(1)(ga) – added by the Noise and Statutory Nuisance Act 1993.

[5] Noise made by traffic, military forces, political demonstrations or demonstrations supporting or opposing a cause or campaign is specifically excluded by section 79(6A). It is also apt to cover noise in streets and public places held not to have been covered by earlier legislation: see *Tower Hamlets London Borough Council v Manzoni & Walder* (1984) J.P. 123 and commentary by Macrory in (1984) J.P.L. 388.

[6] See 1990 Act, section 80A and Schedule 3 brought into force in Scotland on 1 April 1996 by S.I. 1996 No. 186.

6.2.2 Enforcement Procedures

6.2.2.1 Inspection

It is the duty of every local authority to cause its area to be inspected from time to time to deal with statutory nuisances. Where a complaint of a statutory nuisance is made to it by a resident, it must investigate [1].

[1] Failure to carry out this duty may be challenged by means of judicial review, seeking specific performance of statutory duty: Court of Session Act 1988, section 45. The default powers available to the Secretary of State under Schedule 3(4) of the 1990 Act apply only to England and Wales. Alternatively, a complaint may be made to the Ombudsman. There have been a number of such complaints. In *Case 88/A/1864 London Borough Council of Brent* 3 May 1990, the Ombudsman found that there had been a five month delay between the initial visit in response to a noise complaint and the technical evaluation. It was not sufficient to assume that the problem had ceased just because the complainer had not contacted the Environmental Health Department during that period to find out about the progress of the complaint. There was a duty on the local authority to keep the complainer informed, and to keep proper records. In *Case 88/C/1373 Sheffield City Council* 19 September 1989, a delay of 20 months between deciding that a statutory nuisance existed and service of an abatement notice was said to be unacceptable. The local authority was obliged to serve the notice even where it had created or encouraged the nuisance. In *Cases 88/C/1571 and 88/C/182 (Rotherham Metropolitan Borough Council* 26 November 1990), it was found that a failure or excessive delay in responding to 'out of hours' calls in relation to noise nuisance (Sunday clay pigeon shooting) was not acceptable and was a breach of the local authority's duties, even where they were short-staffed. In these cases, where there were a considerable number of complaints, two monitoring inspections in two years was improper. See also report numbers 95/A/4098, 94/A/3062, 95/B/3338, 95/B/1161, 95/A/0615.

6.2.2.2 Power of Entry

Any person authorised by the local authority has substantial powers of entry to premises, vehicles or machinery, either to check whether a statutory nuisance exists or take any action authorised by Part III of the 1990 Act [1]. A warrant to enter may be obtained from a sheriff or justice of the peace in various circumstances [2]. Forcible entry may be made to a vehicle emitting noise (including theft alarms) without warrant if an enforcement notice has not been complied with [3]. It is a criminal offence to wilfully obstruct such right of entry [4].

[1] See 1990 Act, Schedule 3, paragraphs 2 and 3.

[2] Schedule 3(2),(3)

[3] Schedule 3(2A) and sections 79(1)(ga) and 80A

[4] Schedule 3(3).

6.2.2.3   Abatement Notices

Where the local authority are satisfied that a statutory nuisance exists, or is likely to occur or recur, it must serve an abatement notice [1]. The notice specifies the nuisance complained of, what should be done about it and by when [2]. The notice is served on the "person responsible for the nuisance" [3] or on the owner, where the nuisance concerns structural defects in premises. Where the "person responsible for the nuisance" cannot be found, or the nuisance has yet to occur, the notice is served on the owner or occupier of the premises [4]. The person on whom the notice is served must comply with it within any time limit specified. Failure to do so may lead to criminal proceedings. The local authority may also take action to abate the nuisance itself, charging the expenses for doing so to the person responsible [5]. Special procedures for service of an abatement notice exist where the nuisance concerns noise from a vehicle etc., in the street [6].

[1] 1990 Act, section 80(1). The duty is mandatory, that is, the local authority must serve an abatement notice where it is satisfied that a statutory nuisance exists. Thus the decision of the local authority not to serve a notice because it was "not appropriate" was overturned in *R. v Carrick District Council, ex parte Shelley* The Times, 15 April 1996. See, however, *Nottingham District Council v Newton* [1974] I WLR 923, where it was held, in relation to a defective house, that the local authority need not use these statutory powers where they had alternative powers under the Housing Acts.

[2] Section 80(1). Despite the mandatory working, there is apparently no need to specify a minimum period and a very short period will also suffice : *Strathclyde Regional Council v*

Tudhope 1983 SLT 22. Once the notice comes into effect, it remains in force indefinitely. *R. v Birmingham Justices, ex p. Guppy* (1988) 152 JP 159. The form must detail the rights of appeal (see paragraph 6.2.2.4 *infra*). The notice requires to be precise and practicable in its terms: *Strathclyde Regional Council v Tudhope* 1983 SLT 22. In the case of noise nuisance, it has been held that the notice should refer to an objective standard as "the mere fact that witnesses assert that a noise amounted to a nuisance" does not establish its existence: *Greenline Carriers (Tayside) Limited v City of Dundee District Council* 1991 SLT 673 at 675L. Contrast with *Adam (Scotland) Limited v Bearsden & Milngavie District Council* 1996 SLT (Sh. Ct.) 21, where the test of 'audibility' by any 'reasonably minded individual with normal hearing' was *not* objectionable as being subjective. In *Network Housing Association Limited v Westminster City Council* [1995] Env.L.R. 176; (1995) 27 HLR 189 (noise insulation in block of flats), the failure of the notice to specify the nature of the work required (as opposed to the reduction of decibels required) invalidated the notice.

[3] I.e, the person to whose act, default or sufferance the nuisance is attributable (s79(7)). In the case of inadequate sound insulation, this could be the landlord from which the property is rented, *(Network Housing Association Limited, supra)* or the person carrying out works *(Rossall v London Borough of Southwark, supra)*.

[4] Section 80(2)

[5] Both matters are considered below at 6.2.2.5.

[6] See section 79(1)(ga) (car alarms etc.,) and section 80A. Broadly speaking, the notice is to be attached to the vehicle if the person cannot be found.

6.2.2.4 Appeals

A person served with an abatement notice, may appeal to the sheriff within 21 days of the date of the notice [1]. This is done by way of summary application [2]. Even where an appeal is timeously made, a criminal offence will be committed where there is a breach of the notice [3]. It has been held that failure to appeal against a notice deprived the accused of the opportunity to challenge the terms of the notice at a subsequent trial for breach of the notice [4]. Appeal proceedings should be dealt with quickly [5]. Appeal may only be made on one (or more) of ten specified grounds [6]. It is not open to the person appealing the notice to challenge the grounds on which the local authority determined that a noise was in fact a nuisance [7]. At the appeal hearing, it may be sufficient for an environmental health expert to give evidence, rather than the complainer [8].

[1] Section 80(3) Schedule 3, and Statutory Nuisance (Appeals) (Scotland) Regulations 1996 S.I. 1996 No. 1076. The notice itself must specify that appeal can be made and the time limit (1990 Act, Schedule. 3 (6))

[2] Schedule 3 (1A)

[3] Section 80 (4), (5): *Lambert Flat Management v Lomas* [1981] 2 All ER 280. Regulation 3 of the 1996 Regulations (*supra*) provide for very limited circumstances in which the notice may be suspended pending appeal. Even in these limited circumstances, the local authority has the power to prevent the operation of any such suspension : Reg (3)(3).

[4] *Stagecoach Limited v McPhail* 1988 S.C.C.R. 289, a noise nuisance under the (now repealed) Part III of the Control of Pollution Act 1974. The position in England appears to be different: *Sterling Homes (Midlands) Limited v Birmingham City Council* (unrep), Divisional Court, 5 July 1995.

[5] See comments of Sheriff Stewart in *Meri Mate v Dundee District Council* 1994 SCLR 960 at 962 B–F.

[6] See 1996 Regulations, *supra*, regulation 2.

[7] *J C Campbell & Partners v Inverclyde District Council,* (unrep.) 15th March 1981, Greenock Sheriff Court, Sheriff Young, noted at 1994 SCLR 964.

[8] *Cooke v Adatia* (1989) 153 JP 129, 1989 CLY 2784.

6.2.2.5 Non-compliance with abatement notice

Where an abatement notice has not been complied with, various remedies are available. Failure, without reasonable excuse, to comply with an abatement notice, is a criminal offence [1]. "Reasonable excuse" is not defined [2]. There are various statutory defences available [3]. In addition, the local authority may, whether or not criminal proceedings are commenced, abate the nuisance themselves [4]. Special procedures for abatement are provided in respect of noise emitted from vehicles etc. in the road [5]. The local authority is entitled to recover the costs of abating the nuisance themselves [6]. If the local authority is of the opinion that bringing criminal proceedings against a person who has contravened an abatement notice would be an inadequate remedy, it may bring interdict proceedings in the Sheriff Court or Court of Session [7].

[1] Section 80(4). On conviction, the maximum fine is level 5 on the standard scale (£5,000) together with a further fine of one tenth of that fine per day during which the offence continues after conviction. The maximum fine in respect of offences committed on industrial, trade or business premises is £20,000: Section 80 (5),(6).

[2] In *Wellingborough District Council v Gordon* (1991) JPL 874, The Times, 9 November 1990, it was held that the holding of a birthday party was not a reasonable excuse for noise nuisance. Lack of finance was not an excuse in *Saddleworth Urban District Council v Aggregate and Sand* (1970) 114 S.J. 931. Where premises are in such a state as to constitute a statutory nuisance (section 79(1)(a)) simply removing the occupants may not constitute abatement of the nuisance: *Coventry City Council v Doyle* [1981] 1 WLR 1325. The defence is not available where there has been deliberate contravention of the notice: *Lambert Flat*

Management Limited v Lomas, supra. In England, it has been decided that the relevant date for deciding whether the nuisance has been abated and the notice obeyed is not the date of the court hearing but the date on which the information was laid (i.e. date of commencement of criminal proceedings): see *Coventry City Council v Doyle, supra,* and *Lambeth London Borough Council v Stubbs* [1980] J.P.L. 517. But see *Johnson's News of London Limited v Ealing Borough Council,* The Times, 28 July 1989, where the opposite view was taken.

[3] See section 80(7) which provides that, (subject to subsections 8 and 9), it shall be a defence to show that the best practicable means were used to prevent or counteract the effects of the nuisance. See section 79 (9) for definition of best "practicable means".

[4] Section 81(3) and Schedule 3.

[5] Section 80A. The person authorised by the local authority may break into the vehicle and/or remove it.

[6] Section 81(4). The sheriff may apportion expenses between the persons responsible for the nuisance. In Scotland, unlike England, the expenses cannot be secured by a legal charge on premises (s81A (10)).

[7] Section 81(5). It is irrelevant that there is an abatement notice in force or that the local authority has itself suffered no loss as a result of the nuisance. The title and interest of the local authority in this case is as an environmental or public health authority and not landlord (even if it happens to be the owner of any premises on which a nuisance is occurring). This avoids the type of problems encountered in *Dundee District Council v Cook* 1995 SCLR (N) 1995 discussed above at 4.3. For examples of use of injunctions to stop parties, see Municipal Journal Nos. 35, 37 and 39. See also *Hammersmith London Borough Council v Magnum Automated Forecourts* [1978] 1 All ER 401; [1978] 1 WLR 50 (CA). In *Cumnock & Doon Valley District Council v Dance Energy Associates* (unrep.) Ayr Sheriff Court 1st June 1992 (1992 GWD 25–1442), the holding of a rave was held not to be likely to cause inconvenience 'beyond a reasonable level of tolerance', and accordingly interdict was refused. Also material to the decision was that few people were likely to be affected, that it was a 'one-off' event, and that the organisers had attempted to mitigate the nuisance by offering alternative accommodation to residents in the vicinity.

6.2.2.6   Action by person affected by nuisance

Where a nuisance is alleged to exist, any person affected by it would usually report the matter to the environmental health department of the local council (the local authority). In addition, or alternatively, a person who is "aggrieved [1] by the existence of a statutory nuisance" may make a summary application to the sheriff under section 82 of the Act. Prior to commencing court proceedings, the aggrieved person must serve a written notice on the person responsible giving his/her intention to bring proceedings if the statutory nuisance is not removed [2]. The notice and any subsequent proceedings are generally served on the person responsible for the nuisance [3]. That person may be the local authority [4]. The proceedings are civil not criminal [5]. If the sheriff is satisfied that the alleged nuisance exists, or is likely to recur on the same premises or road, the sheriff must make an order to deal with the nuisance [6]. The sheriff does not have the power to order compensation or to fine the defender [7]. Contravention of such an order without reasonable excuse is a criminal offence [8]. Where a defender has been convicted or if the defender cannot be found, the sheriff may order the local authority to do anything in the order to which the conviction relates [9]. If the sheriff is satisfied that the nuisance exists and makes the premises unfit for human habitation, the sheriff may prohibit the use of the premises for human habitation until the premises are, to the satisfaction of the sheriff, rendered so fit [10]. Expenses incurred by the applicant in the court proceedings must be awarded against the defender where the nuisance is proved to have existed at the date of making the summary application [11].

[1] The "person aggrieved", must have some personal interest in the statutory nuisance complained of, but the definition should be a wide one : *Att.-Gen. (Gambia) v N'Jie* [1961] AC 617, [1961] 2 All ER 504 at 511 and *Cumming v Secretary of State for Scotland* 1992 SCLR 831(IH). See for example *Sandwell Metropolitan Borough Council v Bujok* [1990] 3 All ER 385. The person aggrieved is not prevented from pursuing the other legal remedies at the same time, for example, for damages: *R. v Highbury Corner Magistrates Court ex parte Edwards* [1994] Env.L.R. 215.

[2] Section 82(6). There is no specified form of notice. There is no requirement in s82 to specify what works require to be done; that is for the sheriff to determine if the statutory nuisance is proved. But see *Warner v Lambeth London Borough Council* (1984) 15 IILR 42. The period of notice given must be at least 21 days (unless the nuisance relates to section 79 (1)(g) or (ga) (noise nuisance)) in which case the notice period is 3 days.

[3] Section 82(4)(a). Where the nuisance relates to a structural defect, it is served on the owner; where the person responsible cannot be found, it is served on the owner or occupier of premises; where it is noise emitted from an unattended vehicle etc, it is served on the person responsible for the vehicle etc.

[4] In England, where this procedure has been available for some time, local authorities are frequently cited as defendants, particularly in relation to defective housing stock. See for example *Sandwell Metropolitan Borough Council v Bujok* [1990] 3 All ER 385.

[5] Unlike in England where the procedure is criminal in nature (due to the power of the court to impose fines where a statutory nuisance is found to exist). The standard of proof therefore, in England is beyond all reasonable doubt whereas in Scotland, the standard is the civil standard: on the balance of probabilities. See, for example, *Botross v London Borough of Hammersmith and Fulham* (1994) 27 HLR 179.

[6] Thus, an order may only be sought where the nuisance already exists, and not in its anticipation (unlike the power of the local authority to serve a notice in the case of an anticipated nuisance). The order will be for one or both of the following purposes. Firstly to require the defender to abate the nuisance within a specified time and to carry out any necessary works. Secondly, prohibiting recurrence of the nuisance and requiring any necessary works to be carried out within a specified time to prevent the recurrence. The order must be precise and specific in its terms: *Wright v Kennedy* 1946 JC 142 at 146.

[7] Unlike in England where the defendant may also be fined, and a compensation order made under section 53 of the Powers of Criminal Courts Act 1973. The term 'defender' rather than respondent is used in the Act in relation to Scottish proceedings.

[8] Section 82(8) and see 6.2.2.5 notes 1, 2 and 3.

[9] After having given the local authority the opportunity to be heard : section 82(11), (13).

[10] Section 82(3). This is a question of fact. Non-compliance with any statutory requirements or standard does not necessarily mean that the premises is unfit : *Birchall v Wirrall Urban District Council* (1953) 117 JP 384. There is a substantial quantity of literature and cases relating tounfitness for human habitation. See for example annotations to section 113 in *Watchman (1989), Housing Scotland Act 1987, W. Green & Son;* Brown & McIntosh *(1987) Dampness and The Law, Shelter and Legal Services Agency;* O'Carroll & McIntosh *(1993), Solicitors Dampness Action Pack , Legal Services Agency.*

[11] Section 82(12).

6.3   Noise and Statutory Nuisance Act 1993.

Loudspeakers and Burglar Alarms

This Act amended parts of the 1990 Act [1]. It also introduced provisions relating to loudspeakers in roads [2] and burglar alarms. The provisions relating to loudspeakers in roads apply to an area only if the local authority has made an order to that effect. The provisions allow the authority to consent to the use of a loudspeaker, the use of which would otherwise be a contravention of section 62 of the Control of Pollution Act 1974 (other than for electoral or commercial advertising). Section 9 and Schedule 3 relate to the common nuisance of burglar alarms which sound for no good reason. It provides increased powers to deal with such nuisance but has not yet been brought into force [3].

[1] Which amendments, where relevant, are noted in paragraph 6.2 *supra.* Certain parts, including those noted here, apply to Scotland: sections 8 and 13.

[2] Schedule 2.

[3] As at 30 September 1996.

6.4 Noise Act 1996

This Act applies only to England and Wales. Where a local authority has passed a resolution, it may bring into effect provisions in the Act prohibiting noise during the night under pain of a fixed penalty fine [1]. The local authority is also given the power to seize equipment used to make noise unlawfully which may also be confiscated [2]. There are no proposals to extend the Act to Scotland.

[1] Sections 2 to 9.

[2] Section 10 and Schedule.

7 RECOVERY OF POSSESSION: NOTICES OF PROCEEDINGS AND NOTICES TO QUIT

Court action for eviction should be preceded by service of one or more notices on the tenant. The form and procedure for service of these notices differs depending on the type of tenancy, and there is often little margin for error. Failure to comply with these formalities may lead to the court action being dismissed.

7.1 Types Of Tenancy

Most residential tenancies are now governed by statute [1]. Most of the few remaining common law tenancies will be those which are specifically excluded from statutory protection [2]. It is essential to be clear at the outset what type of tenancy the tenant has [3]. This may not always be obvious [4].

[1] Secure tenancies (mostly council housing and older housing association tenancies) are governed by the Housing (Scotland) Act 1987 ('the 1987 Act'), especially Part III, sections 44 to 84A. Protected tenancies (private tenancies created prior to 2nd January 1989) are governed by the Rent (Scotland) Act 1984, Parts I and II. Assured and short assured tenancies (private and most new housing association tenancies created after 2nd January 1989) are governed by the Housing (Scotland) Act 1988, Part II.

[2] For example, those tenancies referred to in Schedule 2 of the 1987 Act, and in particular lets to homeless persons, local authority employees, and secure tenants decanted to permit repairs to their principal homes. Some tenants with resident landlords may also be common law tenants: see Paul Brown *Resident Landlords* SHLN No. 13 (November 1990), page 21. See also the position of some hostel dwellers who may acquire tenancy rights Mike Dailly, '*Ejection Brevi Manu and Hostel Dwellings*' (1995) JLS 435.

[3] On the question of determination of the nature of the tenancy, see Jonathan Mitchell, *Eviction and Rent Arrears* (Shelter 1995), Chapter 2.

[4] See, for example, *Campbell v Western Isles Islands Council* 1989 SLT 602 (creation of secure tenancy in house let to homeless persons in fulfilment of statutory duty); *Burrows v Brent London Borough Council* [1995] EGCS 128 (creation of new secure tenancy by operation of law following delay in seeking warrant to evict and acceptance of rent).

7.2 Common Law Tenancies

7.2.1 A common law tenant has no security of tenure. If the period of the lease has expired, the landlord need not justify to a court his reason for seeking to evict the tenant. He need only comply with certain legal formalities as regards procedure [1]. If the period has *not* expired, the landlord must show that a material condition of the lease, whether express (for example, a clause prohibiting nuisance) or implied (for example the duty to take reasonable care of the premises) has been breached. If it has, and there is an irritancy clause [2] giving the landlord the right to terminate the lease following such a breach, the tenant has no protection from eviction if the breach is proved.

[1] Unless he has contractually fettered his right to recover possession by specifying that he will only do so on certain grounds: see *Lambeth London Borough Council v McLaren* (unrep.) 1st February 1995, Wandsworth County Court, LAG, March 1995, page 11; see also *Clays Lane Housing Co-operative v Patrick* (1984) 17 HLR 188.

[2] An irritancy is 'the forfeiture or determination of a right consequent upon an omission to comply with, or an act done in contravention of, the express or implied conditions upon which the particular right is held'. See Paton and Cameron, *Landlord and Tenant* (Greens 1967), page 228. Where the condition is express, the irritancy is termed 'conventional'; where implied (for example, a failure to pay rent) the irritancy is termed 'legal'.

7.2.2 Common law tenancies are brought to an end by means of a notice to quit (or 'notice to remove'). There is no set form of words [1], but the notice must be a 'definite and unconditional intimation, enabling the other party to know exactly his position so as to be free to make other arrangements' [2]. A demand, therefore, to remove 'if necessary' would be insufficient to terminate a valid lease, as might a 'request' to remove [3]. Apart from a valid notice to quit, no further documentation need be served on the common law tenant, prior to initiating the court action itself.

[1] Unlike that required to terminate an assured or protected tenancy: see paragraphs 7.4.2 and 7.5 below.

[2] *Murray & Anr v Grieve* (1920) 36 Sh Ct Reps 126 at 127.

[3] *Hamilton District Council v Maguire* 1983 SLT (Sh Ct) 76.

7.2.3 The notice should be served no less than 28 clear days prior to the specified date of removal [1]. If the lease is for four months or less, and is silent on the question of the period of notice, then the period will be one third of the term of the lease or 28 days, whichever is greater [2]. If the lease is for more than four months, 40 days' notice will be required [3], again unless excluded by the terms of the lease. If the lease is for a year or more, then 40 days will always be required for the notice [4]. If there is no written lease, and no agreement as to the length of the lease, the law will imply that it will last one year [5].

[1] Rent (Scotland) Act 1984, section 112; *Dumbarton District Council v Sweeney* (unrep.) 13th August 1981, Dumbarton Sheriff Court.

[2] Removal Terms (Scotland) Act 1886, section 5.

[3] Sheriff Courts (Scotland) Act 1907, section 38.

[4] Sheriff Courts (Scotland) Act 1907, section 37; *Shetland Islands Council v BP Petroleum Development* 1990 SLT 82, 1989 SCLR 48.

[5] *Gray v University of Edinburgh* 1962 SC 157, 1962 SLT 173. See, however, *Scottish Residential Estates Development Company Ltd v Henderson* 1991 SLT 490 (occupancy held to be a licence rather than a lease).

7.2.4   A notice to quit may be served for one of two reasons. The first is to prevent the lease tacitly relocating (i.e. automatically renewing itself on expiry). The second is to found an action of removing (for example, that the tenant has breached a condition of the lease relating to anti-social behaviour) [1]. Where the notice is for the first purpose, the period, whether 28 days, 40 days, or otherwise, must coincide with the ish – the last day of the tenancy. If the tenant has breached the lease and the landlord has the express or implied right to irritate, it may be terminated at any point during its term on giving the appropriate period of notice. The failure to remove from the property on the date specified by the notice to quit gives the landlord the right to commence court proceedings. This will be an action for removing and ejection, if the lease has come to an end, or declarator of irritancy and ejection if the lease is being terminated prematurely. In *Hamilton District Council v Maguire,* supra, the sheriff was not prepared to assume, in the absence of averments, that the notice to quit was served for the second purpose rather than the first. As the date of removing specified by the notice did not coincide with the ish, the action was dismissed.

[1] Paton and Cameron, *Landlord and Tenant* (2nd ed), p. 272.

7.3   Secure Tenancies

7.3.1   The termination of secure tenancies is governed exclusively by section 46 of the Housing (Scotland) Act 1987. In particular, in an action for recovery of possession, it is the order of the sheriff that terminates the contractual tenancy [1] and not a notice to quit, which is not therefore required. A 'Notice of Proceedings for Recovery of Possession' must, however, have been served on the tenant before any court action has been commenced [2]. This is a statutory form [3]. There is no margin for error in its construction. It is not, however, a 'substitute' for a notice to quit, but serves a different legal function. On one level it is a 'shot across the bows', or final warning, to the tenant. On the other, it is a necessary first step in commencing court proceedings for recovery of possession. Invalid notices of proceedings are regularly served by local authorities.

[1] 1987 Act, section 46(1)(e).

[2] 1987 Act, section 47(2).

[3] Secure Tenancies (Proceedings for Possession) (Scotland) Order 1980, SI 1980/1389.

7.3.2   The notice of proceedings must specify the ground, being a ground set out in Part I of Schedule 3 to the 1987 Act, on which proceedings for recovery of possession are to be raised [1]. Although this section seems to suggest that only one ground may be specified and that a separate action is required for each ground, this is not in fact the case [2]. The landlord can only subsequently seek to prove the ground or grounds which are specified in the notice. It cannot be amended later [3]. This is because the notice is a creation of statute (which makes no provision for error), and not a requirement imposed by the court rules [4].

[1] 1987 Act, section 47(3)(a).

[2] Interpretation Act 1978, section 1(2): the single includes the plural and vice versa, unless otherwise specified.

[3] Unlike the similar notice in relation to repossession of assured tenancies see paragraph 7.4.5 below.

[4] Summary Cause Rules 1976, section 5 provides that the sheriff has the power to release any party from what would otherwise be the consequences of failing to comply with the court rules, where there has been a 'mistake, oversight or other cause not being wilful non-observance' of the rules.

7.3.3   In *Midlothian DC v Tweedie* [1], the pursuers served a notice of proceedings on the tenants specifying ground 1 of Schedule 3 to the 1987 Act (a breach of a term of the tenancy agreement). They were successful in showing that the tenants' sons had been guilty of anti-social behaviour, and obtained decree for eviction at proof. However, although there was a clause in the lease prohibiting anti-social behaviour, this prohibition was against such behaviour by the tenants only, and not 'other persons residing with them' such as their sons. A letter sent with the notice which suggested that ground 7 was also to be founded upon, did not rectify the failure of the notice itself to specify ground 7. Accordingly the pursuers had no evidence to substantiate a claim under ground 1 that 'an obligation of the tenancy had been broken.' The pursuers were not permitted to amend their notice to specify ground 7, which would have caught behaviour by the tenants' sons, and accordingly their action was dismissed on appeal. The sheriff principal reached the decision 'with regret' but criticised the 'at best slipshod and careless' approach of the pursuers in preparing the statutory documents.

[1] (Unrep.) 3rd March 1993, Edinburgh Sheriff Court, Sheriff Principal Nicholson (1993 GWD 16–1068).

7.3.4 The mode of service of the notice must conform to statute [1]. This may be by personal service, leaving it at the tenant's last known address, or by recorded delivery post to the last known address. Again, as this is prescribed by statute, there is no margin for error. Ordinary post is insufficient, and the onus will remain on the landlord to prove service by one of these methods, so, for example, lost or mislaid certificates of posting are likely to prove fatal to a rigorously defended case. Such things tend not to be noticed until court proceedings are well advanced. Where there are joint tenants, the notice must be addressed to, and served on, each of them [2].

[1] 1987 Act, section 84.

[2] See *Newham London Borough Council v Okotoro* (unrep.) 23rd November 1992, Bow County Court, LAG, March 1993, page 11. It was held in this case that the tenant in section 83 of the (English) Housing Act 1985 meant both tenants, even where one of them had in fact left the house. This would also be the position in Scotland – 1987 Act, section 47(2)(a) read with section 82.

7.3.5 Section 47(3)(b) of the 1987 Act requires that the notice specifies:

'a date not earlier than 4 weeks from the date of service of the notice, or the date on which the tenancy could have been brought to an end by a notice to quit had it not been a secure tenancy, whichever is later, on or after which the landlord may raise proceedings for possession.'

The date specified on the notice is not the date on which the landlords actually raise court proceedings, but the date on which they may do so. Accordingly it matters not that a subsequent court action has been raised at a date consistent with the other strictures of section 47(3)(b) if the date specified in the notice is wrong. In the second place, it is clear that in no circumstances can the relevant date be less than four weeks from date of service. This apparently simple arithmetical calculation causes regular problems for landlords' solicitors overly anxious to raise proceedings against allegedly unruly tenants. It is submitted that the phrase 'not less than four weeks' means 'not less than four *clear* weeks', or put simply, that there must be 28 days between the date on which the tenant receives service, and the date specified in the notice, *not including either* of those two dates [1]. So if the tenant receives service on the 1st of the month, and the date in the notice specifies the 29th of the month as the date on or after which proceedings may be raised, it is arguable that the notice will be incompetent, and any subsequent court action will be liable to be dismissed.

[1] See, for example, *MacMillan v HMA* 1983 SLT 24; *Wilson, Petr* (1891) 19 R 219.

7.3.6 Notwithstanding the four week period referred to in section 47(3), the relevant date to be specified in the notice will be still *later* than this if the tenancy could not have been terminated by means of a notice to quit within that period. This is an unusual provision given that notices to quit are not required for termination of secure tenancies. It has been argued that this means that the date specified in the notice must always coincide with the ish [1]. This argument was apparently accepted by Sheriff Stoddart in dismissing the case of *Renfrew District Council v Armitt* [2].

[1] Jonathan Mitchell, (1995) *Eviction and Rent Arrears*, Shelter Scottish Housing Law Service, paragraph 3.3.

[2] (Unrep.) 23rd February 1995, Paisley Sheriff Court.

7.3.7 The notice of proceedings remains valid for a period of six months only from the specified date on or after which the landlord may raise proceedings [1]. This means that the landlord must raise proceedings against the tenant within this six-month period or the notice will expire and a fresh notice will have to be served in order to commence court action. 'Raising proceedings' means 'commencing an action by effectual citation' – the tenant must actually have been properly served with the court summons in order for the action to be considered to have commenced [2]. The requirement to raise proceedings within the time limit cannot be waived simply because the tenant agrees to such a waiver [3]. This apparently simple matter is sometimes overlooked by local authorities. For example, in

Dundee District Council v Robertson [4], the notice was served on 12th October 1992, and the action raised on 21st May 1993. The pursuers statement of claim even narrated within it the date of the service of the notice.

[1] 1987 Act, section 47(4).

[2] *City of Edinburgh District Council v Davis* 1987 SLT (Sh Ct) 33.

[3] *Ridehalgh v Horsefield and Another* [1994] 3 WLR 462, [1994] EGCS 15 and [1992] EGCS 45.

[4] (Unrep.) (Case H6041/93), 6th February 1995, Dundee Sheriff Court.

7.4 Assured Tenancies

7.4.1 In order to terminate the lease and raise proceedings for recovery of possession of an assured tenancy, it is likely that *both* a notice to quit and a statutory notice must be served.

7.4.2 Notice to Quit

Unlike the common law notice to quit, certain prescribed information must be given to the tenant in addition to the unconditional notice to remove [1]. Section 18(7) of the 1988 Act provides that the sheriff may make an order for possession of a house let on a contractual tenancy which has been terminated. By contrast, section 16(3) provides that where the assured tenancy has been terminated, and a statutory assured tenancy has been created, no further notice to quit is provided. This suggests that a notice to quit is still required in general to end the contractual tenancy [2].

[1] Assured Tenancies (Notice to Quit Prescribed Information) (Scotland) Regulations 1988, SI 1988/2067: Form AT6.

[2] This is also the advice given to tenants on Form AT6.

7.4.3 Section 18(6), however, suggests that no notice to quit is required at all if the landlord seeks to establish (amongst others) one of the 'conduct' grounds of Schedule 5 to the Act – grounds 13 and 15 – and the terms of the tenancy make provision for it to be 'brought to an end on the ground in question'. What is meant by this is not entirely clear. It may imply something along the lines of a conventional irritancy clause [1], rather than merely an option on the part of the landlord to seek to terminate the lease.

In other words, a provision like:

'This lease shall be terminated if the tenant is convicted of using drugs in the premises'

might mean that no notice to quit need be served if indeed that conviction has been obtained [2]. The safest option for landlords remains to serve a notice to quit anyway. In the case of *Edinvar Housing Association v Graham* [3], the sheriff dismissed the pursuers' case on the grounds that a notice to quit had not been served, that such a notice was required and that the tenancy agreement did not provide for the tenancy to be brought to an end on the ground of the tenant's behaviour. Accordingly the action was dismissed as incompetent.

[1] On the nature of conventional irritancy clauses, see paragraph 7.2.1 above.

[2] There is authority for the proposition that no notice to quit is required at common law if the action of removing is 'extraordinary', i.e. to enforce an irritancy of the lease: *MacDougall v Guidi* 1992 SCLR 167; *Pickard v Reid* 1953 SLT (Sh Ct) 5.

[3] (Unrep.) 24th March 1995, Edinburgh Sheriff Court, Sheriff Bell.

7.4.4 In any event, raising proceedings on the only other ground relevant to the tenants conduct (ground 9 – the compulsory transfer ground), being specifically excluded from section 18(6), will certainly require a notice to quit.

7.4.5 Notice of Proceedings

Notwithstanding whether a notice to quit requires to be served, a notice of proceedings for possession should be served before an action of recovery of possession will be competent [1]. The formalities of this notice are rather less stringent than those required for secure tenancies. The notice referred to is statutory Form AT6 [2]. However, notwithstanding the detail of the form and the clarity with which it gives notice and advice to the tenant, the sheriff may dispense with the requirement of service of the form altogether if he considers it 'reasonable' to do so [3]. In addition, the sheriff may permit alteration of the Form AT6 to change or add to the ground specified [4]. Accordingly any error or incompetence on the part of the landlord in completing or serving this notice can be rectified at the discretion of the sheriff. This discretion is unfettered and serious anti-social behaviour on the part of the tenant may be one reason for dispensing with service of a proper notice. This does have the unfortunate consequence that a tenant might conceivably be brought to court (and evicted) without having had either a notice to quit or a statutory notice served on him to warn him of impending proceedings.

[1] 1988 Act, section 19(1)(a).

[2] Assured Tenancies (Forms) (Scotland) Regulations 1988, SI 1988/2109.

[3] 1988 Act, section 19(1)(b). In *Kelsey Housing Association v King, The Times*, 8th August 1995, CA, the judge held that it was reasonable to dispense with the notice given the developments since the commencement of the proceedings, and the late stage at which objection to the deficiency of the notice had been taken. In refusing the tenant's appeal, the court held that the judge could have regard, in dispensing with notice, to matters arising after the raising of the action.

[4] 1988 Act, section 19(2). See, however, *Mountain v Hastings* (1993) 25 HLR 427, *The Times*, 1st April 1993, (CA), where a notice under section 8 of the (English) Housing Act 1988 failed to 'state fully' the text of the ground for recovery. This requirement is also present in the Scottish notice – see SI 1988/2109 Form AT6, Part 2. The ground of recovery was the 'mandatory' three month rent arrears ground (in Scotland, ground 8 of Schedule 5 to the 1988 Act). The landlords had failed to notify the tenant that the ground could not be made out if less than three months' rent was still due at the date of the hearing. The action for recovery was dismissed.

7.5 Protected Tenancies

There is no system of statutory notices in respect of tenancies under the Rent (Scotland) Act 1984. However, a notice to quit will be required at not less than 28 days' notice which must contain the information prescribed by regulation [1]. The considerations in relation to periods of notice in relation to common law leases referred to in paragraph 7.2.3 above will therefore apply.

[1] Rent (Scotland) Act 1984, section 112; Notices to Quit (Prescribed Information) (Protected Tenancies and Part VII Contracts) (Scotland) Regulations 1980, SI 1980/1667.

8 RECOVERY OF POSSESSION: COURT PROCEDURE AND FAIR NOTICE

Different types of court cases involve different sets of court rules. Almost all cases seeking eviction of anti-social tenants will use summary cause procedure in the sheriff court. In exceptional cases, ordinary cause procedure may be used instead. Failure to comply with the rules of court may lead to the action being dismissed. Particular attention must be paid to whether fair notice of the basis of the action has been given to the tenant.

8.1 Introduction

Nearly all actions for recovery of possession of heritable property (including those seeking the eviction of anti-social tenants) must be commenced under summary cause procedure in the sheriff court [1]. The only exception to this is where payment of more than £1,500.00 (for example, unpaid rent, or damage to the subjects of let), exclusive of interest and expenses, is also sought [2]. In these circumstances, the case must be commenced under ordinary cause procedure. However, this exception may not apply to recovery of possession of secure tenancies [3]. Thus the great majority of anti-social tenant cases will be brought under summary cause procedure [4].

[1] Sheriff Courts (Scotland) Act 1971, section 35(1)(c).

[2] *Monklands District Council v Johnstone* 1987 SCLR 480.

[3] 1987 Act, sections 46(1)(e), 47(1). In *City of Glasgow District Council v Everson* (unrep.) 5th August 1992, Glasgow Sheriff Court, Sheriff JK Mitchell, it was held that the remedy of irritancy was incompetent against a secure tenant. The implication of this, if correct, may be that where it is sought to evict a secure tenant and to sue for payment of more that £1,500.00, two separate court actions will be required.

[4] Accordingly this text focuses primarily on summary cause procedure. This is governed by the Summary Cause Rules (SCR) 1976. No person advising or representing tenants or landlords in eviction proceedings should do so without being fully conversant with these rules. They are amended from time to time, and therefore an up-to-date copy is essential. Duly authorised and 'suitable' lay representatives other than solicitors or advocates may represent tenants in proceedings under these rules, but only at the first calling of the case or any subsequent calling where 'the cause is not defended on the merits' (Summary Cause Rule 17). Summary cause procedure is also well detailed in MacPhail (1987), *Sheriff Court Practice*, Greens, Chapter 25, although this chapter is now slightly out of date (see, for example, paragraph 8.4,n2 below). See Mays (1995), *Summary Cause Procedure in the Sheriff Court*, Butterworths, for a detailed exposition of the rules.

8.2 Ordinary cause

Two forms of ordinary cause action may be available when seeking to evict an occupier: removing and ejection [1]. An action of removing is appropriate where the occupier is a tenant. Characteristically the action will also seek a declarator that the tenancy has come to an end and has not tacitly relocated. Where the action is as a means to enforce an irritancy, and hence to bring the lease to a premature end, the action is termed an 'extraordinary removing'. 'Warrant to eject' the tenant will also be sought [2]. This should be distinguished, however, from an action of ejection. This latter court action is appropriate where the occupier has no right or title to occupy the premises, his occupation being by fraud, force or precarious possession [3].

[1] Ordinary procedure in the sheriff court is governed by the Ordinary Cause Rules 1993 (Schedule to the Sheriff Courts (Scotland) Act 1907, (as amended)). Only solicitors or advocates may represent tenants being sued for eviction under these rules. The rules of ordinary cause procedure detailed in MacPhail, *Sheriff Court Practice* are the pre-1993 Rules and accordingly the book is severely out of date in this respect, although on many points of principle it remains invaluable. See also paragraph 8.1, n3: ordinary cause procedure may not be available for actions involving secure tenancies.

[2] This being the accessory proceedings used by the successful pursuer to allow him to physically remove an occupier of the property who refuses or delays to quit the premises notwithstanding the court order to do so.

[3] Paton and Cameron (1967), *Landlord and Tenant,* Greens page 284. The terminology is confused yet further by the use of the phrases 'summary warrant of ejection' and 'warrant for summary ejection' in sections 36 and 37 of the Sheriff Courts (Scotland) Act 1907. As has been commented, the law on recovery of possession is in an 'unsatisfactory' state (Scottish Law Commission Report No. 118, *Recovery of Possession of Heritable Property* (HMSO Cm 724, (1989) paragraph 1.2).

8.3 It is competent for an eviction action to include a crave for interdict. Such an action would have to be under Ordinary cause procedure [1]. The interdict could be directed at further neighbour nuisance by a tenant in an action of removing, or against continued occupation, in an action of ejection, against an anti-social occupier without right or title to remain.

[1] Interdict is not one of the prescribed proceedings which may be brought as a summary cause in terms of section 35(1) of the Sheriff Courts (Scotland) Act 1971. It is thought that this also precludes composite actions, i.e. suing for both eviction and interdict in the same action: SLC Report No. 118, supra, paragraph 8.10.

8.4 Summary cause

Summary cause procedure begins with lodging, warranting and service of a summons on the defender [1].   Rule 2 of the Summary Cause Rules provides that:

> '2(1) There shall be annexed to the summons a statement of claim which shall give the Defender fair notice of the claim ...'

Although written averments in summary cause procedure do not have to pass the stringent tests of relevancy and specification present in ordinary cause, the defender must still be given 'fair notice' of the case which s/he has to meet, in order to prepare his defence [2].   Failure to comply with rule 2 will render the summons incompetent and liable to be dismissed [3].

[1] Normally approximating, as nearly as is practicable, to Summary Cause Rules Form C (where the action is for recovery of possession only). Where the action is for recovery of possession and payment, e.g. of rent arrears, a 'variable' summons will be used: Sheriff Courts (Scotland) Act 1971, section 36(2); Summary Cause Rule 1.

[2] 'However summary a cause may be, there can be no departure from the rules of fairness and these include the necessity to give fair notice to one's opponent of the case which he has to meet': *Roof Care Ltd v Gillies* 1984 SLT (Sh Ct) 8 *per* Sheriff Principal Bennett at page 9. 'The summary cause pleader does not require to present a case which can pass a relevancy test prior to proof. He only requires to give reasonable notice of his case and he ought also to bear in mind that it is in the essential nature of the summary cause procedure that the defender may not be legally represented.' *Visionhire Ltd v Dick* (unrep.) 18th September 1984, Kilmarnock Sheriff Court, Sheriff Principal Caplan (noted in MacPhail, *Sheriff Court Practice*, paragraph 25.23n). Note that MacPhail's treatment of this subject relates to the rule prior to amendment into its present form in 1993. In particular, there is now explicit reference to 'fair notice' in rule 2, rather than just an inference that it should be present.

[3] *Gordon District Council v Acutt* 1991 SLT (Sh Ct) 78 at 80 D - E; MacPhail, *Sheriff Court Practice* at paragraph 25.23n, quoting Sheriff MacInnes in *Birds Eye Foods Ltd v Johnston* (unrep.) 3rd February 1977, Cupar Sheriff Court.

8.5 'Fair notice' is a flexible concept [1]. The landlords' agents should, however, give a clear indication in the written statement of claim of the specific allegations on which they intend to found at proof.   It is unacceptable, and ultimately self-defeating, to purposely attempt to do anything else.   Nevertheless, some landlords' agents have been prepared to go to proof on a statement of claim which makes no more than a bald averment that 'the tenant has been guilty of anti-social behaviour', without making any further specification of what the tenant is supposed to have done. This may seem to some landlords' agents a useful means of 'ambushing' the unrepresented tenant [2]. The disadvantage of the use of such tactics is that, even if the statement of claim passes the basic test of competency in terms of the Summary Cause Rules, any evidence led at a proof on matters not sufficiently specified in the statement of claim may be open to objection. If the objection is repelled, this may give grounds for appeal. The whole point of written court pleadings is to clarify those points on which the parties 'agree to disagree'. Failure to do this means that the whole legal process may be lengthier and more expensive.

[1] See MacPhail, *Sheriff Court Practice*, paragraph 9.29: the degree of specification sufficient to constitute fair notice will depend on the circumstances, which will be considered broadly by the court - *McMenemy v James Dougal and Sons Ltd* 1960 SLT (N) 84.

[2] This is particularly the case given that the defender has no power to compel the landlord to disclose the names of witnesses to allow precognition before proof. Nor is there any provision in the summary cause rules to challenge the other party's written pleadings prior to proof (short of want of jurisdiction or obvious incompetency: Summary Cause Rule 18(4) and 18(7)). There are also special difficulties in the not uncommon situation where the allegations are wholly or mainly against third parties (for example, the tenant's children) who may have other reasons for not disclosing fully to the tenant's solicitor.

8.6 In giving fair notice, rule 2 requires that the statement of claim

'shall, in particular, include ... details of the basis of the claim including any relevant dates'.

The 'basis of the claim' will be adequately specified from an express or implied reference to the grounds of the 1987 Act upon which the landlord intends to found. There should also be a reference to the existence and service of the notice of proceedings. There must also be a narration of 'any relevant dates'. In the case *Motherwell District Council v Mary McLoughlin or Burns* [1], the pursuer's statement of claim contained a large number of generalised allegations relating to the defender's behaviour but failed to specify any dates on which the incidents were supposed to have occurred. The action was dismissed, therefore, as being incompetent through failure to comply with rule 2. In the case of *Motherwell District Council v Stark* [2], a different view was apparently taken [3]. However, it is submitted that the central point of *Burns* was correctly decided. It is not about *specification* of dates, but about the *competency* of the action if no dates are narrated in the statement of claim. If there are, as a matter of law, dates which are 'relevant' (as decided by the sheriff), then it is mandatory for the pursuer to include at least one of them in his statement of claim in order to satisfy the test of competency. It is hard to conceive of any anti-social eviction case where at least one of the dates of an alleged incident would not be 'relevant'. Failure to aver *any* dates, therefore (as in *Burns*), can render the action incompetent, and (subject to amendment - see paragraph 8.11 below) liable to be dismissed.

[1] (Unrep.) 15th February 1994, Hamilton Sheriff Court, Sheriff MacPherson.

[2] (Unrep.) 31st October 1994, Hamilton Sheriff Court.

[3] See letter from Mr D. Ross 1995 JLS 10.

8.7 It is unlikely, however, that a statement of claim will be rendered incompetent where there are a series of incidents, some dated and others not. This argument was apparently addressed in *Motherwell District Council v Stark,* supra. For example, a statement of claim might narrate that:

'the tenant had an unacceptably loud party on 3rd February 1990, and has in the four years since then had five other noisy parties'.

To dismiss such a statement of claim as incompetent would involve reading the word 'any' in rule 2(1)(a) to mean 'all'. The competency of the statement of claim falls to be judged as a whole. However, this is a separate matter from that of specification of dates. Failure to sufficiently specify when an incident happened may lead to a successful objection to the leading of evidence [1]. It is submitted that the degree of specification required will depend on the individual circumstances of the case and in particular the nature and frequency of the incidents and the reasonable possibility of providing specification [2]. It may, of course, be highly relevant to the question of reasonableness as to when the incident occurred, in relation to the date of the hearing itself.

[1] Where a party seeks to lead evidence on matters not contained in the statement of claim, their opponent may object to it being led. The sheriff may uphold or reject the objection, or permit the evidence to be led subject to further consideration of its competency and relevancy at the conclusion of the proof. Lodging documents as productions does not amount to giving fair notice in the statement of claim, unless these are properly referred to and copies produced: *Birds Eye Foods Ltd v Johnston* (unrep.) 3rd February 1977, Cupar Sheriff Court, quoted in MacPhail, *Sheriff Court Practice*, paragraph 25.23.

[2] Therefore it might be both competent and perfectly specific to aver, for example, 'the tenant had five noisy parties in March and April 1993'; competent but inspecific to aver, for example, 'the tenant had a noisy party on one occasion in 1993' and incompetent to aver only 'the tenant has repeatedly encouraged his dogs to foul the common green'.

8.8   In addition to factual averments in relation to the ground for eviction, there should also be averments as to reasonableness [1]. Absence of any written averment that it is reasonable to make the order has been held to render the action incompetent [2]. In some cases, however, the court will be prepared to infer that it is reasonable that decree be granted without there being any written averment to this effect [3]. In such a case, that inference can only be drawn from the actual ground of recovery itself or possibly from the procedural history of the court case [4]. Similarly, if the statement of claim does make a specific averment, following narration of alleged facts, 'that it is therefore reasonable to evict', this too means that only the proved facts of anti-social behaviour can support the landlords contention that it is reasonable to evict. In *City of Glasgow District Council v McDonald* [5], the pursuer sought recovery of possession on the ground of the tenant's alleged anti-social behaviour. The sheriff held that it followed from *Erhaiganoma* that where:

> 'the pursuer is intent in founding his view that it is reasonable to make an order on facts other than, or beyond, the actual grounds of recovery, the defender should be given some notice of these facts'.

[1] 1987 Act, section 48(2); 1988 Act, section 18(4); Rent (Scotland) Act 1984, section 11(1). *City of Glasgow District Council v Erhaiganoma* 1993 SCLR (N) 592 at 593 F – G. The merits of reasonableness are discussed at Chapter 12 below.

[2] *Renfrew District Council v Inglis* 1991 SLT (Sh Ct) 83.

[3] *City of Glasgow District Council v Erhaiganoma*, supra.

[4] For example, a history of repeated but ineffectual adjournments of the case to permit the tenant's conduct to improve.

[5] (Unrep.) 26th April 1993, Glasgow Sheriff Court, Sheriff Galt.

8.9 Accordingly, unless the actual anti-social behaviour proved against the tenant is so heinous as to infer that it is reasonable to evict, then failure to aver other matters bearing on reasonableness may lead to the failure of the action. For example, a statement of claim might narrate:

> 'The tenant has repeatedly had noisy parties which have caused nuisance and annoyance to neighbours. It is therefore reasonable that the order for possession be granted'.

On the face of it reasonableness may be inferred from the pleadings. If, however, the tenant is able to show that but for the failure of the landlord to provide adequate noise insulation the neighbours would not have been caused nuisance or annoyance, this may rebut the presumption of reasonableness. On the landlord's present pleadings, however, any attempt to lead evidence to show, for example, that the tenant had failed to respond to the landlord's requests for mediation with neighbours, or that he had alternative accommodation to live in were he to be evicted, would be open to objection.

8.10 Where the action is brought seeking to establish nuisance and annoyance against a secure tenant [1], there must also be material before the court to establish that it is reasonable for the landlord not to offer alternative accommodation. There should accordingly be averments specifically directed towards this question. In practice this may amount to nothing more than: 'If the tenant were transferred, he would continue to behave in an anti-social fashion'. However, the facts of the case would have to be such as to clearly demonstrate that the behaviour complained of was not linked to the specific housing situation, be it the physical condition of the house itself, or the particular relations between the tenant and his neighbours [2]. The action will not, however, be rendered incompetent by a failure by the pursuer to amplify a simple averment 'that it is not reasonable to make other alternative accommodation available' [3]. The same facts adduced by evidence may, however, be sufficient for the purpose of establishing reasonableness under section 48(2) and 'unreasonableness' under ground 7 of the 1987 Act.

[1] I.e. in terms of ground 7 of Schedule 3 to the 1987 Act. This discussion has no application to assured or protected tenancies, there being no direct equivalent to ground 7 in these Acts. See further paragraph 10.2.5 below.

[2] See *Dundee District Council v Heggie* (unrep.) 14th January 1991, Dundee Sheriff Court, Sheriff Stewart and paragraph 12.5 below.

[3] *Western Isles Islands Council v Smith* (unrep.) 31st October 1994, Stornoway Sheriff Court. However if, as *per City of Glasgow District Council v McDonald* above, the pursuer chooses not to amplify this averment, he may be restricting the evidence which he will be entitled to lead and found on in inviting the sheriff to find this part of ground 7 established. It must be remembered, however, that the onus of proof remains with the pursuers: reasonableness is a mixed question of fact and law. There must be at least some evidence on which the pursuers are entitled to rely. If the defender denies that it is not reasonable to not give him another house, then the pursuers are not entitled to rely on an inference from an absence of evidence to the contrary: for example, that there was 'no reason to believe that the tenant would behave better if rehoused elsewhere'.

8.11 A failure to comply with the terms of rule 2 of the Summary Cause Rules may lead an action to be held incompetent, and dismissed. If a defect is discovered, however, there is provision made in the rules for amendment of the statement of claim so as to cure the incompetency [1]. If the party wishes to amend less than seven days prior to the proof, however, he will have to show 'special circumstances' justifying his failure to do so up to that point. This is not just a matter of whether the amendment would or would not cause prejudice to the tenant. In *Scottish Homes v Hamilton* [2], an action for recovery of possession was dismissed on appeal after the sheriff had allowed amendment of the summons following the conclusion of the proof. In *City of Glasgow District Council v McDonald,* supra, leave to amend was refused at the commencement of the proof. But 'special circumstances' is a flexible concept and leaves considerable discretion for the sheriff. In *Link Housing Association v Spence* [3], an amendment was allowed, after hearing of evidence, which led to the dismissal of the action, notwithstanding the sheriff's suggestion that the defenders solicitor 'apparently only bothered to prepare his case the day before'.

[1] Summary cause Rule 27; *Gordon District Council v Acutt* 1991 SLT (Sh Ct) 78 at 80 G – H.

[2] 1993 SCLR 771.

[3] (Unrep.) 12th June 1993, Edinburgh Sheriff Court, Sheriff Scott. The case concerned tenants lying to obtain an assured tenancy. The notice to quit purported to give 28 days' notice, but in fact did not. The original written statement of defence relied on reasonableness. After allowing amendment of the defence, the sheriff held that the notice to quit was invalid and that the action should be dismissed. No written judgment was issued.

8.12 Remit to the Ordinary Roll

The summary cause procedure is ill suited to actions for recovery of possession in neighbour nuisance cases. At stake is a tenant's home, and their future right to public housing, for both themselves and their dependants. Summary cause procedure is, however, intended to be quick and relatively unconstrained by legal formality. It is often inherent in the nature of anti-social conduct cases that the landlord will wish to lead lengthy and detailed evidence of alleged misconduct stretching back over months if not years. There is, however, no procedural mechanism in a summary cause whereby the tenant can require the reluctant landlord to specify exactly on which alleged incidents he wishes to found. While there are often difficult points of law which arise in tenant conduct actions, there is no procedure in a summary cause which permits the tenant to challenge the legal relevancy of the landlords case [1] prior to hearing of the evidence [2]. Such mechanisms do, however, exist in ordinary cause procedure.

[1] Short of obvious incompetency or want of jurisdiction; SCR 18(4).

[2] SCR 18(7).

8.13 Section 37 of the Sheriff Courts (Scotland) Act 1971 provides that a summary cause can be remitted to the ordinary roll [1] either on the joint motion of the parties, or on the motion of one party only. If the motion is joint, the sheriff must remit the case; if it is one party's motion only, he may do so at his discretion. In an action for recovery of possession of heritable property, the sheriff may also remit the case ex proprio motu (unilaterally). The sheriff may remit the cause if 'he is of the opinion that the importance or difficulty of the cause make it appropriate to do so'. The only two reported cases on the question of 'appropriateness' both concern actions for recovery of possession. In *Hamilton District Council v Sneddon* [2], there were allegations of misconduct made against the housing officers involved in the recovery action which might, in the view of the sheriff principal, have made the case of sufficient 'importance' for the remit to be made. In *Hart v Kitchen* [3], the failure to seek remit was severely criticised. It was held that there was clearly a question of the competency of the action and a remit to the ordinary cause would have allowed a debate on the point. Indeed the court indicated that the defender's solicitors were at fault in not seeking to do so.

[1] I.e. changed from a summary cause action to an ordinary cause.

[2] 1980 SLT (Sh Ct) 36.

[3] 1990 SLT 54.

8.14 In neighbour nuisance cases where complex issues of fact or law arise, such a motion should be made. If the remit is sought on the grounds of a point of competency, then the agreement of parties to the motion may be in both landlords and tenant's interest. Summary Cause Rule 18(7) provides that no question of law can be determined by the sheriff until after determination of the facts. It is clearly in no-one's interests to hear possibly several days of evidence at a proof just for a case to be dismissed as legally incompetent. While the sheriff may retain a common law power to entertain an argument as to competency prior to proof, this is more likely to be the case where the point is one of fundamental nullity, rather than of degree [1]. Unless the parties agree, it is for the particular sheriff to determine whether the remit is appropriate, and the refusal to do so is not open to appeal [2]. In a neighbour nuisance eviction case, issues of legal complexity, the volume of evidence and numbers of witnesses might all make a remit appropriate.

[1] *Hart v Kitchen,* supra, at page 57 I – J; on the interaction between the summary cause rules and the residual common law powers of the sheriff in recovery actions generally, see MacPhail, *Sheriff Court Practice* (Greens 1988), paragraph 2.09; *City of Edinburgh District Council v Robbin* 1994 SLT (Sh Ct) 51, SCLR 43; *Pyle and Pyle v Christie and Christie* (unrep.) Edinburgh Sheriff Court, 1993, Sheriff Principal Nicholson.

[2] 1971 Act, section 37(3).

8.15 Suspended Possession Orders

8.15.1 In terms of section 20(2) of the Housing (Scotland) Act 1988, the sheriff, on making an order for possession of an assured tenancy, may sist or suspend execution of the order for such period or periods as he sees fit. He may also impose such conditions as he sees fit to the sist or suspension. If these conditions are not breached, the sheriff may subsequently recall the order. The authors know of no reported decisions. In the case of *Govanhill Housing Association v Isobel Mackenzie* [1], nuisance and annoyance was proved against the tenant, caused almost entirely by her alcoholism. It was also held to be reasonable to grant the order. In suspending the order for possession for two months, the sheriff 'was satisfied that in order to stop the defenders present behaviour she required to obtain treatment for her alcohol dependency [and] in my judgment some form of compulsitor was [therefore] necessary'. The conditions imposed on the tenant were that she undertook such treatment for alcoholism as determined by her social workers; that she caused no further disturbance, nor allowed other persons into her flat likely to do so; that a positive report on her progress be provided by the social work department; and that the landlords be given an opportunity to be heard as to whether any further complaints had been received from neighbouring tenants [2].

[1] (Unrep.) 7th July 1995, Glasgow Sheriff Court, Sheriff Peebles.

[2] Mr Mackenzie is apparently still the tenant (at June 1997).

8.15.2 There is no directly equivalent provision for secure tenancies in the 1987 Act [1]. The sheriff does, however, have the power in terms of section 48(1) to adjourn proceedings for a period or periods and impose conditions. This underused power may enable the court to confine the threat of eviction to the 'guilty' parties in neighbour nuisance situations. In *Dundee District Council v Rice* [2], the sheriff imposed conditions that the tenant not reside at the house with her cohabitee, the real source of complaint, and that she take all reasonable steps to prevent him visiting. Alternatively the power has been used by the sheriff to attempt to persuade the unwilling landlord to reconsider making alternative accommodation available [3]. Where nuisance and annoyance of one kind has been established at proof prior to adjournment, further proof establishing other types of nuisance at a continued proof may be considered together with the first, both in establishing the ground and the question of reasonableness. In *Dundee District Council v Anderson* [4] the tenant's son had caused nuisance and annoyance by playing football, and by cheek and abuse of elderly neighbours. After a six-month adjournment, decree was granted when further proof established that the son in question had 'progressed' from insolence to violence, and had been joined in this by his brother. The power to adjourn is, however, only available where proceedings are brought under grounds 1 to 7 of Schedule 3 to the 1987 Act [5]. A motion for adjournment is by no means automatically granted, however [6].

[1] Unlike in England where suspended possession is regularly granted in anti-social behaviour cases.

[2] (Unrep.) 8th October 1991, Dundee Sheriff Court, Sheriff Raeburn.

[3] *Dundee District Council v Westwater* (unrep.) 11th May 1995, Dundee Sheriff Court, Sheriff Eccles; *Dundee District Council v Heggie* (unrep.) 14th January 1991, Dundee Sheriff Court, Sheriff Stewart (decision upheld before Sheriff Principal Maguire, 14th August 1991); *Clackmannan District Council v Morgan* (unrep.) 22nd October 1991, Alloa Sheriff Court, Sheriff Younger. In the latter two cases the refusal of the landlords to consider rehousing led to refusal of the order for possession following the adjournment.

[4] (Unrep.) 8th September 1993, Dundee Sheriff Court, Sheriff Macfarlane; 3rd February 1995, Dundee Sheriff Court, Sheriff Principal Maguire.

[5] So, for example, proceedings which are solely for compulsory transfer (ground 8) may not be adjourned in terms of this rule.

[6] For example, *Western Isles Islands Council v Smith* (unrep.) 31st October 1994, Stornoway Sheriff Court: 'having regard to the persistent and grave nature of the conduct which is a nuisance and of which I have found the defender to be guilty, and his past failings to heed warnings and implement assurances, I was not remotely persuaded that there was any merit in the [motion to adjourn].'

9 RECOVERY OF POSSESSION: GROUNDS FOR RECOVERY OF COMMON LAW TENANCIES

There are few common law tenancies in Scotland. They are governed by the terms of the lease agreement, and by other terms implied by common law or statute. Some implied terms may be relevant to neighbour disputes.

9.1 Common law tenancies [1] are governed by the terms of the lease and those terms implied by law. Common law terms may, unless specifically excluded by the lease, also be implied into secure, assured or protected tenancies. This is a matter of reading the lease itself – if not expressly excluded, the common law will be included. There is, however, no implied term at common law that a tenant not act in an anti-social fashion towards his or her neighbours [2]. Apart from the obligation to pay rent, the law generally recognises the following implied terms which may be relevant to neighbour disputes [3].

[1] There are few common law tenancies in Scotland – see paragraph 7.1. However, the proposals for probationary tenancies may significantly alter this picture: see Chapter 14.

[2] Although it has been suggested that a possible law reform would be to have such a term implied by statute – see paragraph 14.4.

[3] In practice these are frequently made express in written lease agreements.

9.2 The tenant has a duty to enter into and continue in possession of the subjects of let [1]. A tenant who ceases to occupy the house for a long period or abandons the house will be in breach of lease. This duty is for most practical purposes superseded by statute for non-common law tenancies [2].

[1] Paton and Cameron, *Landlord and Tenant*, pages 135–6; Rankine, *Leases*, page 233.

[2] Housing (Scotland) Act 1987, sections 46(1)(d), 49–51, 55; Housing (Scotland) Act 1988, section 23(1).

9.3 The tenant has the duty not to invert possession [1]; that is, the tenant must only use the premises for the purposes for which they were let. Accordingly, if the subjects of the lease are let for use as a residential dwelling, it will be a breach of lease to use them to carry on a business.

[1] Paton and Cameron, page 137; Rankine, page 236.

9.4 The tenant has a duty to take reasonable care of the subjects of let [1]. Failure to do so will give grounds for an action of damages and if sufficiently serious, there may be an implication that the tenant has breached the lease and the landlord will be entitled to terminate it.

[1] Paton and Cameron, page 138.

10 RECOVERY OF POSSESSION: GROUNDS FOR RECOVERY OF POSSESSION OF SECURE TENANCIES

An order for recovery of possession of a secure tenancy can only be made on one of the grounds set out in Part 1 of Schedule 3 to the Housing (Scotland) Act 1987. There are 16 grounds, of which the first eight relate in varying measure to the conduct of the tenant. Grounds 1 to 7 are discretionary: the sheriff may only order possession if he is satisfied that in addition to the ground being established, it is also reasonable in all the circumstances that the order be granted. Grounds 8 to 16 are mandatory: if established, the sheriff must grant the order. In practice, grounds 1 and 7 are the most important and are considered first. Grounds 2, 3, 4 and 8 which are of relevance to nuisance cases are also examined.

10.1 'Ground 1: Rent lawfully due from the tenant has not been paid, or any other obligation of the tenancy has been broken.'

10.1.1   This text is not concerned with the question of rent arrears. It is, however, competent to seek in the same action to recover possession on grounds of rent arrears and anti-social behaviour [1]. All secure tenancies must be constituted by a written lease [2]. It must be drawn up by the landlord, and executed prior to the commencement of the tenancy [3]. The National Consumer Council found in 1976 that 94% of local authority lease agreements contained some form of prohibition on unsocial behaviour. The most recent estimate is around 97% [4]. The form of such 'nuisance clauses' varies widely, however. In some, the clause is narrower than the nuisance ground for recovery provided by statute [5]. Many other tenancy agreements seek to broaden the statutory grounds substantially [6].

[1]   A variable summons would not be required unless a decree for payment is also sought. On defences to actions for non-payment of rent in secure tenancies, see Jonathan Mitchell, *Eviction and Rent Arrears* (Shelter Scottish Housing Law Service 1995).

[2]   1987 Act, section 53(1) as amended by the Requirements of Writing (Scotland) Act 1995. The lease need no longer be probative or holograph, but simply subscribed: Requirements of Writing (Scotland) Act 1995, section 2(1).

[3]   1987 Act, section 53(2). A few tenants who have resided in the same council house since before the coming into force of the Tenants' Rights etc. (Scotland) Act 1980 may still not have a written lease.

[4]   Clapham et al. (1995), paragraph 11.8 (69 out of 71 councils).

[5] I.e. 1987 Act, Schedule 3, ground 7 – see *Midlothian District Council v Tweedie* (unrep.) 3rd March 1993, Edinburgh Sheriff Court, Sheriff Principal Nicholson; 1993 GWD 16–1068 and paragraph 7.3.3 above.

[6] For example, see *London Borough of Lewisham v Simba-Tola* (1991) 24 HLR 644. Note also that the terms of the Supply of Goods and Services Regulations 1995 apply to tenancy agreements. These may be used to strike down unreasonable terms: see LAG, August 1995, page 24.

10.1.2   The question of the interaction between statutory and contractual terms was considered in *SSHA v Lumsden* [1]. The sheriff principal held that the mere existence of a term of the lease relating to anti-social behaviour less stringent than that provided by statute did not prevent the landlord seeking an order based on another statutory ground. He left open the question as to whether the lease could contractually restrict the landlord's right to use the other statutory grounds. There seems no reason why not. This may occur for policy reasons in some other forms of tenancy [2]. In practice it is highly unlikely that any local authority would wish to do so in relation to anti-social behaviour. Nevertheless, the contractual term must not be inconsistent with or contrary to statutory provision [3], nor can the landlord attempt to contract out of the statutory provisions for recovery [4].

[1]   1984 SLT (Sh Ct) 71.

[2]   The preferred policy of the Scottish Federation of Housing Associations is that the 'mandatory' rent arrears ground – ground 8 – of Schedule 5 to the Housing (Scotland) Act 1988 should be expressly excluded from housing association assured tenancy agreements. However, since in terms of section 16, terms of the contractual assured tenancy relating to termination fly off on the creation of a statutory assured tenancy, there is some doubt as to whether such a restriction would be entirely effective.

[3]   *Artizans, Labourers and General Dwellings Company Ltd v Whitaker* [1919] 2 KB 301. For example, the lease could not provide that a personal, as opposed to tenancy, obligation contained in the lease could permit recovery under ground 1: see paragraph 10.1.6 below.

[4]   *Monklands District Council v Johnstone* 1987 SCLR 480.

10.1.3   The landlord of a secure tenancy can extend the ambit of the grounds for recovery by contractual means. There are two main reasons for this. In the first place, it is useful for tenants to have clear notice of what behaviour is not acceptable in relation to their tenancy. As they are in most cases unlikely to have access to a copy of the 1987 Act, setting this out in the lease agreement has obvious advantages. A prohibition on racial harassment of neighbours, for example, is unlikely to add much to the provisions in the statute, for it is hard to conceive of such conduct not being caught by ground 7 in particular [1]. It can, however, give notice to the tenant of the gravity with which a landlord views such behaviour, and of its policy of seeking possession where racist behaviour is found to exist.

[1] See, for example, *Birmingham County Council v X* (unrep.) 26th October 1992, Birmingham County Court, LAG, March 1992, pages 11–12; *Leicester County Council v X and X,* Inside Housing, 26th March 1993.

10.1.4 Secondly, a widely drawn anti-social clause may assist the landlord in obtaining an order for possession. It is not uncommon for leases to make it clear that the tenant will be liable to be evicted for anti-social behaviour, nuisance or annoyance caused by casual guests or visiting relatives, and to specify that such behaviour will be a breach of the lease if directed towards housing officers or other local authority employees [1]. Further examples include requirements not to keep any pets [2]; or alternatively to 'ensure at all times that any pets kept on the premises do not by their behaviour cause any nuisance, annoyance or inconvenience to neighbours' [3]; or to 'not permit to be done anything which may increase risk of fire' [4]; to make no structural alterations or additions without consent [5]; or to keep the subjects of let in 'clean neat and tidy condition and in good order' [6].

[1] See *Govanhill Housing Association v O'Neil,* infra at paragraph 10.2.4.1; *London Borough of Lewisham v Simba-Tola,* supra. See paragraph 10.2.1.6 below.

[2] *Green v Sheffield City Council* (1994) 26 HLR 349.

[3] *Basildon District Council v Tugwell* (unrep.) 7th July 1993, Brentwood County Court, LAG, March 1995, page 11.

[4] *Wandsworth London Borough Council v Hargreaves* (1995) 27 HLR 142.

[5] *Glenrothes Development Corporation v Graham* (unrep.) 14th December 1994, Kirkcaldy Sheriff Court, Sheriff Patrick.

[6] Ibid.

10.1.5 Care must be taken in drafting such clauses. For example, if a number of specific examples of prohibited behaviour are given, it should be made clear that these are not exhaustive of what constitutes anti-social behaviour. Otherwise the law may imply that other types of conduct do not constitute such behaviour [1]. For example, if a lease were to contain a clause such as:

'The tenant shall not conduct himself in an anti-social manner towards his neighbours. A tenant shall be guilty of anti-social conduct if he causes excessive noise at anti-social hours, or is racially abusive to neighbouring tenants.'

Such a prohibition may mean that excessive noise at *non* anti-social hours, or racial abuse of neighbouring tenants' *family or friends* does *not* constitute a breach of the lease. Where there is ambiguity in a deed, its interpretation by the court may be made against the interest of the person who drew it up, i.e. in this case the landlord [2]. Accordingly, if the landlord wishes a term of the lease to be qualified or restrictive in its terms, this should be clear. In *Williamsburgh Housing Association Ltd v McLeod* [3], for example, it was held that permission in the lease to keep a 'dog' meant any dog, and not just the particular animal owned by the tenant at the time the condition was made. In order to determine what, if any, obligation is intended to be created by a clause, it must, however, be considered as a whole and in its context [4].

[1] *Expressio unius est exclusio alterius* – i.e. the particular mentioning of one thing operates to exclude other things different from it.

[2] The doctrine of interpretation *contra proferentem* – i.e. against the person from whom it proceeds.

[3] (Unrep.) 8th December 1987, Paisley Sheriff Court, Sheriff Principal Caplan (1988 GWD 2-77).

[4] *Scottish Wholefoods Collective Warehouse Ltd. v Raye Investments Ltd and Barclays Bank plc* 1994 SCLR 60, IH *per* Lord McCluskey at page 64.

10.1.6 The anti-social clause, however written, will only be of assistance to the landlord if it creates an obligation *of the tenancy*. Not everything written in a lease agreement will create such an obligation: 'it must be binding on the tenant as tenant and not merely something binding on him as an individual ... the words are not "obligation of the tenant", but "obligation of the tenancy" ... it does not become so merely because those words are inserted in the agreement' [1]. The temptation, for example, might be to attempt to include a clause in the lease to the effect that the tenant

'will be in breach of the lease if he is convicted of any offence related to or constituted in whole or in part by racial harassment.'

Such a condition may be unenforceable in terms of the tenancy. It involves no connection between the prohibited conduct and the occupation of the house, and reads more as a policy statement about the kind of tenants that landlord wishes to house, than about the quality of the occupancy.

[1] *RMR Housing Society Ltd v* Combs [1951] 1 KB 486 at 491 *per* Singleton LJ, distinguishing *Marquis of Bute v Prenderleith* 1921 SC 281. See also *Scottish Society for the Prevention of Cruelty to Animals v MacLeod*, (1944), 60 Sh Ct Reps 183. These cases concerned occupiers who were also employees, and where the landlords sought to show that the occupancy was dependent on continuing employment. The occupiers sought to show that a lease had been created notwithstanding that the house had been let to an employee. It was significant to the tenant's successful defence in *RMR Housing Society Ltd v Combs* that he was employed by someone *other than* the landlord.

10.1.7 The question of what constitutes a 'breach of an obligation of the lease' does not appear to have been considered by the courts in Scotland in relation to anti-social tenants. It has, however, been considered in other contexts. In *Govanhill Housing Association v McKibbens & Malley* [1] the defender had lied in order to induce the landlord to grant her an assured tenancy. The tenancy agreement contained a clause in which the defender declared the truth of her prior statements. The landlords attempted to show that the false statement inducing the landlord to grant the lease was an 'obligation of the lease' [2]. The defender argued that as the false statement was made prior to entering into the lease, it could not be in breach of an obligation of it. The sheriff held [3] that the tenant had breached an express warranty of the lease to the effect that she would not make misleading statements. He held that this was sufficient to establish the ground for possession [4].

[1] (Unrep.) 25th April 1994, Glasgow Sheriff Court, Sheriff Evans.

[2] There being no equivalent ground to ground 6 of the 1987 Act in the Housing (Scotland) Act 1988. Ground 6 of Schedule 3 to the 1987 Act provides that recovery of possession may be granted where 'the landlord was induced to grant the tenancy by a false statement made knowingly or recklessly by the tenant'. On what might not constitute a 'false statement', see *Peterborough County Council v Moran* (unrep.) 11th June 1993, Peterborough County Court, LAG, September 1993, page 13.

[3] Under reference to Gloag on *Contract*, page 466.

[4] It was, however, also held not to be reasonable to grant the order.

10.1.8 Ground 1 may be used to seek recovery following breach of both express obligations written in the lease and obligations implied into the lease at common law [1]. Implied obligations may, however, be expressly excluded by the lease.

[1] *Robertson v Wilson* 1922 SLT (Sh Ct) 21. On relevant common law implied terms, see Chapter 9 above.

10.1.9   Where there is a conventional irritancy clause [1] in the lease, and the tenant breaches the obligation, the irritancy cannot later be purged (i.e. the breach repaired) unless the landlord has acted oppressively [2]. For example, if a lease stipulates that the landlord may terminate the lease if the tenant keeps a dog in the house and the tenant does so, he will still be in breach of the lease even if at the date of proof he has got rid of it [3]. The question of whether there is repetition of the breach or an intention to continue with it will be material to the question of reasonableness [4].

[1]   See paragraph 7.2.1, n 2.

[?]   *Stewart v Watson* (1864) 2 M 1414; *Dorchester Studios (Glasgow) Ltd v Stone and Another* 1975 SLT 153; *CIN Properties Ltd v Dollar Land (Cumbernauld) Ltd* 1992 SLT 669, 1992 SCLR 820, HL. This does not, incidentally, apply to the obligation to pay rent on a secure tenancy: if the tenant has cleared the rent arrears at the time of the hearing, decree may not be granted: *Gordon District Council v Acutt* 1991 SLT (Sh Ct) 78 at 80 B – E.

[3]   Or to fail to repair and decorate the house and cultivate the garden: *Brown v Davies* [1958] 1 QB 117.

[4]   *Bell London and Provincial Properties v Reuben* [1947] KB 157; *Green v Sheffield City Council* (1994) 26 HLR 349.

10.1.10   The landlord cannot raise proceedings based on ground 1 if he has acquiesced in or condoned the breach. To show acquiescence, it is not sufficient for the tenant merely to show that the landlord was aware of the breach. Acceptance of rent by the landlord after he has become aware of a breach may not imply acquiescence [1]. Rather there must be actions amounting to 'unequivocal affirmance' of the state of affairs following the breach so as to clearly imply that the landlords have waived their statutory rights to seek recovery [2]. This is a matter of fact and circumstance in the individual case [3].

[1]   *Oak Property Company Ltd v Chapman* [1947] KB 886. See also *Solihull Metropolitan Borough Council v Reeman* (unrep.) 28th March 1994, Birmingham County Court, LAG, June 1994, page 10, discussed in paragraph 10.2.3.9 below.

[2]   Ibid. at page 900 *per* Somervell LJ. See also *HMV Fields Properties Ltd v Bracken Self Selection Fabrics Ltd* 1991 SLT 31, IH, 1990 SCLR 677: Do 'the landlord's actings in accepting the rent from the tenant who remains in possession, if looked at objectively provide a clear indication that he is willing that the contract should remain in force' (*per* Lord President Hope at page 34 J – K).

[3]   For example, a secure tenant might have a noisy party in contravention of a term of the lease. The landlords write a letter warning that 'any repetition of such conduct may put your tenancy at risk'. The tenant has a further noisy party. It is arguable that in subsequent proceedings for recovery of possession based on ground 1, the landlord would not be entitled to rely on the fact of the first party as constituting a breach of the lease, having implied in the letter to the tenant that no proceedings were to be brought at the time. He may have acquiesced in the breach. This would not prevent him using ground 7, nor from introducing the fact of the first party as regards reasonableness.

10.1.11 Either landlord or tenant has the right to seek to vary the terms of the lease. If the variation cannot be agreed, either may make an application to the sheriff for an order for variation [1]. The tenant may only seek to apply to the sheriff where the term of the lease restricts the tenant's use or enjoyment of the house. This may happen by reason of changes in the character of the house or the neighbourhood making a particular term unreasonable or inappropriate; or because the term is unduly burdensome compared with any benefit resulting from performance; or where the term impedes reasonable use of the house [2]. Such an application will be granted solely at the discretion of the sheriff who must consider whether it would be reasonable to grant it or not, having particular regard to the safety of any person and the likelihood of damage to the house [3].

[1] 1987 Act, section 54.

[2] 1987 Act, section 54(3)(b).

[3] 1987 Act, section 54(4); and see, for example, *Taylor v Moray District Council* 1990 SCLR (N) 551.

10.2 'Ground 7: The tenant of the house (or any one of joint tenants) or any person residing or lodging with him or any sub-tenant of his has been guilty of conduct in or in the vicinity of the house which is a nuisance or annoyance and it is not reasonable in all the circumstances that the landlord should be required to make other accommodation available to him.'

In practice this ground is used for the majority of anti-social eviction cases, whether in isolation or in tandem with other grounds. Its difficult syntax can be broken down into four principal components: the identity of the alleged perpetrator, the nature of the conduct, where it took place, and whether it is reasonable for the landlord not to offer alternative accommodation. It is also appropriate to consider to whom the conduct is directed.

10.2.1 *'The tenant of the house (or any one of joint tenants) or any person residing or lodging with him or any sub-tenant of his ...'.*

10.2.1.1 Tenants and Joint Tenants

The house must be tenanted by a secure tenant. Accordingly, local authority landlords [1] may not use this (or any other) ground in Schedule 3 to the 1987 Act if the tenancy is excluded from being a secure tenancy [2]. For example, if nuisance or annoyance is caused by the occupier of homeless persons' accommodation [3], or a local authority hostel [4], the landlord must rely on the terms of the agreement with the occupier and the common law. It is not competent to obtain decree to recover possession in a 'shared ownership' arrangement (i.e. where the tenant partly owns and partly tenants the house) [5].

[1] And other bodies referred to in section 61(2) of the 1987 Act.

[2] 1987 Act, Schedule 2: broadly these are: lets to employees of the landlord 'for better performance of duties'; temporary accommodation to homeless people; temporary accommodation made available pending development or works to the tenant's principal house; lets of agricultural or business premises; lets by police and fire authorities, and lets of houses which form part of or are within the curtilage of another building not used for housing accommodation.

[3] See, however, *Campbell v Western Isles Islands Council* 1989 SLT 602 where the landlord's failure to expressly let the house on a temporary basis to a homeless person resulted in a secure tenancy being inadvertently created.

[4] See *Thomson v City of Glasgow District Council* 1986 SLT (Lands Tr) 6, where a hostel resident failed to establish that his room was 'let as a separate dwelling' and therefore a secure tenancy which he would have a 'right to buy'. See also Dailly (1995); paragraph 7.1 n2.

[5] *Link Housing Association v McCandlish and Marsh* (unrep.) 1990, Glasgow Sheriff Court, Sheriff McLernan. In such circumstances the landlord's remedy is an action for division and sale: *Langstane (SP) Housing Association Ltd. v Davie* 1994 SCLR (N) 158.

10.2.1.2 Where there are joint tenants, only one need be guilty of nuisance or annoyance. The possible innocence of the other joint tenant or tenants is irrelevant in this context [1]. It is not possible for the innocent joint tenant to seek to 'evict' the anti-social joint tenant by means of an action for recovery of possession [2].

[1] *City of Glasgow District Council v Brown* 1988 SCLR 433 and 679. It may, of course, be highly relevant to the question of reasonableness.

[2] *Reith v Paterson* 1993 SCLR 921.

10.2.1.3 Residing With

The meaning of 'residing with' was considered in the case of *SSHA v Lumsden* [1]. A tenant's wife caused nuisance and annoyance to her neighbours as a result of her drug and alcohol problems. The tenant was in prison at the time. Sheriff Principal Caplan approved the judgment in the English case of *Neale v Del Soto* [2], where it was held:

'the words "residing with" must be given their ordinary popular significance. They do not ... involve any technical import or have some meaning only to be defined by lawyers ... what is contemplated is the case of a dependent child, or whoever it may be, being one of the household'.

Accordingly, it was held that the tenant's wife was 'residing with him'. In some respects the decision appears result based ('If the defender's wife is unable to behave in a reasonable manner without his supervision then it is up to the defender to keep himself out of prison'), but a significant factor in the sheriff principal's reasoning was that the nature of the wife's occupancy of the house did not alter as a result of the tenant going to prison. She did not stop being a member of his 'household'. Accordingly the defender could not say at what point his wife ceased to 'reside with him'. It may be that a person may 'reside with' someone who is detained in a psychiatric hospital [3], or with an estranged wife, staying only at weekends to attempt a reconciliation [4].

[1] 1984 SLT (Sh Ct) 71.

[2] [1945] 1 All ER 191.

[3] *Greenway v Rawlings* [1952] CLY 3009.

[4] *Green v Lewis* [1951] CLY 2860. Here it was apparently held that 'a man can be said to reside where he usually passes the night'; and see also *Wemyss v Wemyss Trustees* 1921 SC 30 *per* Lord Sands at 40: 'it was common ground to both sides that a person does not "reside" where he does not sleep'.

10.2.1.4 In *Midlothian District Council v Byrne* [1], the person alleged to be the cause of the majority of the nuisance and annoyance was the teenage son of the tenant. She claimed that he no longer resided there as she had told him to leave home. At the time of the proof, he was in prison serving a six month sentence. The sheriff found that he was nonetheless residing with the tenant. Evidence was led that he had recently given the tenant's house as a bail address, and also that he had been found sleeping at the house one afternoon after he claimed to have left. The tenant claimed that she had no control over her son's activities, but in the face of such evidence, she was effectively left with the burden of proving that he had a *new* residence elsewhere [2]. In *Dundee District Council v Rice* [3], the tenant's cohabitee was held to be still 'residing with her' at the time of a nuisance by virtue of his continuing to have a set of keys to the house [4].

[1] (Unrep.) 23rd July 1993, Edinburgh Sheriff Court, Sheriff Shiach.

[2] Although being 'resident' implies a degree of permanence in living in a place, it is a matter of circumstances. A person may be resident in more than one place at any time and the absence of a legal entitlement does not prevent residence being established: *Levene v Inland Revenue Commissioners* [1928] AC 217; *Hipperson v Electoral Registration Officer for the District of Newbury* [1985] QB 1060; [1985] 2 All ER 456, CA.

[3] (Unrep.) 8th October 1991, Dundee Sheriff Court, Sheriff Raeburn.

[4] Notwithstanding a finding that they had not cohabited during the previous month and, at the time of the particular incident in question, the cohabitee had entered the house for the purpose of harassing the tenant.

10.2.1.5 Lodgers and Sub-tenants

A secure tenant may not assign, sublet, take in lodgers, or otherwise part with possession of all or part of the house without the landlord's written consent [1]. A contract of lodging 'consists of not only a furnished house or part of a house but also the use of certain articles which are not usually delivered over in a furnished house and the benefit of certain services in attendance, cooking, bedmaking, shoe cleaning and the like' [2]. A subtenancy is a tenancy granted by the tenant over part or all of the subjects of which he himself is tenant. Were a tenant to purport to take in a lodger *without* the landlord's consent then that person is likely to fall within the category of someone 'residing with' the tenant for the purposes of ground 7. The same might be true where the tenant purports to sublet *part* of the house without consent. However, if the tenant sublets all the house without consent and moves out, the new occupier may not be caught by ground 7 and the appropriate ground for recovery would be in respect of the tenant's breach of obligation of the lease [3], seeking warrant to eject the occupier as a person having no right or title to remain.

[1] 1987 Act, section 55(1), Schedule 4.

[2] Rankine, *Law of Leases in Scotland* (3rd edition), page 288, approved in *Mclaren v Gault* (1917) Sh Ct Rep 216. See also *Street v Mountford* [1985] AC 809; [1985]; *AG Securities v Vaughan, Antoniades v Villiers* [1990] 1 AC 417; *Monmouth Borough Council v Marlog* (1995) 27 HLR 30.

[3] Taking in lodgers or subletting may also be a breach of a contractual obligation not to use premises for business purposes: *Tendler v Sproule* [1947] 1 All ER 193.

10.2.1.6 Ground 7 does not permit recovery based on the acts of casual visitors to the house. There is a clear distinction between residing at and 'paying a visit at a place on invitation' [1]. Accordingly party guests, family or friends staying overnight, and other non-paying guests will not be caught by ground 7. A suitably drafted contractual term in the lease may lead to nuisance and annoyance by such persons being cause for recovery under ground 1.

[1] *Wemyss v Wemyss Trustees* 1921 SC 30 at 42.

10.2.2 *'has been guilty of conduct in or in the vicinity of the house ...'*

'House' includes any part of the building (for example, the common stair or lifts) and in particular any 'yard, garden, outhouses and pertinents belonging to the house' [1]. It means the house where the perpetrator of the conduct resides, not the victim. Precisely what is in the 'vicinity of the house' will depend on the circumstances of the individual case, and the nature of the conduct complained of [2]. Problem cases might include racially abusing a neighbour at the local pub, or street walking in the streets adjoining the house. It is the *conduct*, however, and not the *result* of the conduct, which is geographically limited. Making obscene telephone calls from the house might therefore constitute conduct 'in the house'. Dumping rubbish into a stream or waterway running by the house might be conduct 'in the vicinity of the house', even if the effect was to pollute land elsewhere. 'Guilty' means no more than the acts were knowingly done: the tenant's intention is irrelevant [3]. Where the acts of nuisance were caused by a gang of youths, however, it was not enough to only have a 'considerable suspicion' that the tenant or a member of his family was part of that group: actual involvement must be established on a balance of probabilities [4].

[1] 1987 Act; section 338.

[2] *Whitbread v Ward* [1952] CPL 401; 159 EG 494, CA; *Govanhill Housing Association v O'Neil* 1991 SCOLAG 174.

[3] *Shepherd v Braley* [1981] SCL 150, CA.

[4] *Dundee District Council v Westwater* (unrep.) 11th May 1995, Dundee Sheriff Court, Sheriff Eccles.

10.2.3 *'which is a nuisance or annoyance ...'*

10.2.3.1 The word 'nuisance' has a technical meaning in both English and Scots law. However, in this context it is the ordinary everyday meaning of the word which is relevant. In *Walter v Selfe* [1], nuisance was defined as 'an inconvenience materially interfering with the ordinary comfort physically of human existence, not merely according to elegant or dainty modes and habits of living, but according to the plain and sober and simple notions of English [sic] people'. 'Annoyance' is a broader term than nuisance. In *Tod-Heatley v Benham* [2], it was held that annoyance was 'a thing which reasonably troubles the mind and pleasure ... of the ordinary sensible English [sic] inhabitants of a house ... although it may not appear to amount to physical detriment to discomfort.' This does not make the test subjective: the mere fact that someone has complained, although implying that annoyance has been caused to them, does not establish that the ground is made out. The sheriff has to determine whether the conduct would objectively have annoyed a 'reasonable' neighbour. It does, however, indicate that virtually any conduct is covered, as it is the effect that it has on the complainer which constitutes the nuisance or annoyance, not the nature of the conduct *per se*.

[1] (1851) 20 LJ Ch 433.

[2] (1888) 40 Ch D 80.

10.2.3.2 There does not have to be any course of conduct or repetition – a single act of nuisance or annoyance may be sufficient, if it is particularly serious. In *Govanhill Housing Association v O'Neil* [1], the brandishing of a sword and threatening of another person with it on one occasion was held to establish the ground.

[1] 1991 SCOLAG 174. A decision of the sheriff, later successfully appealed to the Sheriff Principal on a different ground but then overturned by the Inner House of the Court of Session. See paragraph 10.2.4.1 below.

10.2.3.3 The court must consider the circumstances which exist at the time of the hearing. If there has only been one incident and no indication that it will be repeated, it may not be reasonable to grant the order. In *Ottway v Jones* [1], the last act complained of occurred nine months before the hearing. The court refused the order for possession but awarded the legal expenses of the action against the tenant.

[1] [1955] 1 WLR 706, CA.

10.2.3.4 If the court considers the conduct in the context of the standards of the particular neighbourhood, it must do so on the basis of established facts. In *Woking Borough Council v Bistram* [1], possession was sought on the grounds of persistently foul and abusive language towards the tenant's neighbours. At proof, the judge held such behaviour was 'no doubt very much a common experience' in certain areas and refused the order as unreasonable. This decision was reversed on appeal. It was held that there was no evidence before the judge to allow him to make such a finding, and nor was he entitled to rely on his own knowledge of the particular local area. In any event he had attached insufficient weight to the fact that the nuisance was continuing at the date of proof.

[1] (1995) 27 HLR 1.

10.2.3.5 'Nuisance and annoyance' may include any number of types of conduct, including: use of the house for prostitution [1]; blocking of a water closet and permitting a sink to become blocked and overflow into another tenant's home [2]; systematic discourtesy to neighbour's visitors [3]; persistent abuse of the landlord [4], burglary of neighbouring property [5]. On the other hand, acts which have not been established to constitute nuisance and annoyance include interference with the landlord's attempts to carry out alterations to other parts of the building [6]; occasional discourtesy and unpleasant remarks or behaviour [7]; and simply allowing the premises to smell and become dirty [8].

[1] *Frederick Platts Co Ltd v Grigor* (1950) 66 (1) TLR 859, CA; *Yates v Morris* [1951] 1 KB 77, CA.

[2] *Ferguson v Butler* 1918 2 SLT (Sh Ct) 228.

[3] *Shine v Freedman* [1926] EGD 376, DC.

[4] *Adamson v Fraser* (1944) 61 Sh Ct Reps 132.

[5] *Dundee District Council v Rice*, (unrep.) 8th October 1991, Dundee Sheriff Court, Sheriff Raeburn.

[6] *Nevile v Hardy* [1921] 1 Ch 404.

[7] *Taylor v Battey* [1955] NZLR 637.

[8] *Maciver v Struthers* 1924 SLT (Sh Ct) 15.

10.2.3.6 Noise is the most frequent cause of nuisance complaint [1]. For example, in *Poole Borough Council v Carruthers* [2], the tenant was found to be guilty of incessantly playing Jim Reeves records, which persisted notwithstanding a suspended possession order. In *Clackmannan District Council v Morgan* [3], the tenant caused nuisance by, amongst other things, carrying out DIY at night and the 'frequent noisy playing of darts'.

[1] See Nick Yapp, *Law and Your Neighbours* (1989), page 102; Scottish Office/DOE/Welsh Office joint working party report: *Review of the Effectiveness of Neighbour Noise Controls: Conclusions and Recommendations* (March 1995). If the nuisance caused by the noise is as a result of the lack of adequate soundproofing, it may be that the landlord is in breach of the lease and liable to carry out soundproofing and pay damages: *Duncan v London Borough of Brent* (unrep.) 29th November 1988, Willesden County Court, LAG, June 1989, page 18.

[2] (Unrep.) *Guardian* 12th May 1992, *Independent* 20th January 1994; LAG, September 1993, page 13, June 1994, page 10.

[3] (Unrep.) 22nd October 1991, Alloa Sheriff Court, Sheriff Younger.

10.2.3.7 Racial harassment will generally be regarded as nuisance and annoyance, although many local authority leases also contain express prohibitions of such conduct. The legal difficulties of bringing such cases to court generally involve questions of obtaining witnesses and other evidence [1].

[1] For an example of successful coordinated action, see *Greenwich London Borough Council v Wright* (unrep.) 4th January 1990, Woolwich County Court, LAG, February 1990, page 6, March 1990, page 13.

10.2.3.8 The keeping of pets and other animals is another frequent source of neighbour complaint. This may give rise to nuisance or annoyance on account of smell [1], noise [2], biting and intimidation of neighbours [3], or sanitary concerns [4]. Alternatively it may be the nature of the place where the animals are kept which gives grounds for eviction [5].

[1] *Morrisey v Galer* [1955] 1 WLR 110.

[2] *Solihull Metropolitan Borough Council v Reeman* (unrep.) 28th March 1994 Birmingham County Court; LAG, June 1994, page 10; *Spiders Web v Merchant*, [1961] CLY 6359.

[3] *Glenrothes Development Corporation v Graham* (unrep.) 14th December 1994, Kirkcaldy Sheriff Court, Sheriff Patrick; and see paragraph 10.2.3.10 below.

[4] *City of Glasgow District Council v Carroll* 1991 SLT (Sh Ct) 46, 1991 SCLR 199.

[5] See *Mackenzie v West Lothian District Council* 1979 SC 433, where the aviary constructed by the tenant to keep his large collection of birds was built on the common ground of his and the neighbouring tenancies.

10.2.3.9 The failure to adopt a consistent approach by the landlord to recurring nuisances may affect a court's view of the tenant's conduct. In *Solihull Metropolitan Borough Council v Reeman,* supra, possession proceedings were raised as a result of the nuisance caused by noxious smells and odours that were caused by the tenant's dogs. The order for possession was refused. In particular it was established that although there was a general prohibition imposed by the local authority on keeping pets, 15 other tenants in the same block were in breach of the same condition of their respective leases, but had gone unpunished. In addition, it was apparently also established that the tenant had made efforts to reduce any nuisance caused by the dogs.

10.2.3.10 *Glenrothes Development Corporation v Gordon and Anne Graham* [1]

This now notorious case received widespread publicity during the three week proof in the autumn of 1994. All of the following incidents were found by the sheriff to be proved:

- carrying out a motor repair business from the house
- lighting fires in the garden
- allowing dogs to roam, intimidate and bite neighbours or postmen
- drug use
- obstructing the pavement by parking cars on it
- making excessive noise by playing loud music, or revving car engines
- creating noxious fumes or smoke
- upsetting and spreading around refuse awaiting collection
- intimidation of neighbours
- structural alterations to the house
- failing to maintain the garden
- driving motor vehicles illegally (e.g. drunken driving) in the vicinity of the house
- vandalism of neighbouring properties (e.g. breaking windows)
- vandalism of public street fixtures (e.g. breaking street lights)
- assaults on neighbours, their children, sheriff officers or policemen

- throwing bricks or stones at cars driving past the house
- firing air rifles from the property
- urinating in the garden or in the vicinity of the house
- verbal abuse or threats
- burglary of neighbouring properties
- stretching a wire across the road outside the house with a view to causing traffic accidents
- vandalism and theft from cars parked in the area
- setting fire to neighbour's property (e.g. garden shed) [2]

In her judgment, after noting that ground 7 was established 'several times over,' the sheriff described:

'a course of deliberate conduct ranging from an assault on a two year-old child to the wanton destruction of property and harassment of the elderly' leading to 'considerable distress to many people ... all of whom had done nothing to attract the unwelcome attentions of the Graham family and many of whom were forced to take extreme measures such as giving up their homes or employment, seeking medication for a prolonged period, re-landscaping their gardens, reorganising travel arrangements and, in one case, keeping a child a year behind at school.'

It was also noted that 'why the safeguards which our present system provides failed not only the neighbours ... but also to an extent [the tenants and their children] ... clearly merits further examination' [3].

[1] (Unrep.) 14th December 1994, Kirkcaldy Sheriff Court, Sheriff Patrick.

[2] All of this conduct may be prohibited or regulated by legal action other than eviction.

[3] The conduct complained of related primarily to two of the tenant's children, aged 16 and 12. The case has been used as an example of the need to 'get tough' with allegedly anti-social tenants by reduction of tenants' rights generally (see Chapter 14).

10.2.4   *... to neighbours?*

10.2.4.1 Ground 7 does not specify whether the conduct need be directed at any particular person or persons in order for ground 7 to be made out. In *Govanhill Housing Association v O'Neil* supra, Sheriff Principal MacLeod held that in order for ground 7 to be made out, the nuisance or annoyance would have to be directed at neighbours, and not other persons, such as housing association staff, who happened to call at the house in the course of their legitimate business. The case was appealed by the Association to the Inner House of the Court of Session and the appeal was ultimately not opposed [1]. Accordingly, the sheriff principal's decision has been formally overruled, although no written judgment was issued by the Inner House. However, there is still some force in the sheriff principal's judgment. The relationship between landlord and tenant is set out in the lease between them. The purpose of ground 7 is not to give the landlord another means of management control, but to give him powers to act where third parties are adversely affected by the tenant's behaviour.

[1] The case was apparently settled by joint minute, the tenant by this stage having fallen into arrears of rent.

10.2.4.2 By contrast, the equivalent English legislation on secure tenancies specifically provides that the nuisance ground will be made out where the 'tenant or a person residing in the dwelling-house has been guilty of conduct which is a nuisance or annoyance *to neighbours...*' [1]. Who then is the 'neighbour'? In the case of *Greenwich London Borough Council v McGee* [2], an action for recovery was brought on the grounds of sustained racist abuse of an Asian shopkeeper by the tenant. Although the abuse was established, the order was refused. The tenant lived some 350 yards away from the shop where the abuse had taken place. There was no direct route between house and shop. It was held that, although in a very general way the tenant lived in the neighbourhood of the shop, he was not in fact a neighbour of the shopkeeper. Other problem cases might include making offensive telephone calls or sending hate mail [3]. Directing these at a person in the next street might be different in this context from where the person lived in the next town.

[1] Housing Act 1985, section 84 and Schedule 2, ground 2. Note that the Housing Act 1996 changes this definition to bring the phrasing closer to that applying in Scotland.

[2] (Unrep.) 21st December 1989, Woolwich County Court; LAG, March 1990, page 5. See also *Cobstone Investments v Maxim* (1984) 15 HLR 113, CA.

[3] Although these acts may certainly amount to nuisance or annoyance: see e.g. *Khorasandjian v Bush* (1993) 25 HLR 392.

10.2.5 *"... and it is not reasonable in all the circumstances that the landlord should be required to make other accommodation available to him."*

10.2.5.1 It is this factor which helps distinguish ground 7 from ground 8, discussed below. It is also a separate (and prior) question from that of 'reasonableness' under section 48(2) of the 1987 Act. The landlord must show that the conduct complained of is of a type which would be likely to re-occur in alternative accommodation, or that the conduct complained of was so extreme that the pursuer should not be required to maintain the relationship of landlord and tenant at all. In *Kyle and Carrick District Council v James Currie* [1], it was held that:

> 'the words [in ground 7] "in all the circumstances" have within their
> immediate contemplation, as I apprehend, (i) the nature and extent of
> the nuisance or annoyance and (ii) the personal circumstances of the
> defender. That is not to exclude other circumstances. But (i) and (ii)
> seem to me to be obvious and sensible conclusions to have in mind
> in deciding whether or not it is reasonable that the landlord should be
> required to make other accommodation available. The worse the
> nuisance or annoyance, the more likely that it is not reasonable that
> other accommodation should be made available. But straitened or
> difficult circumstances of the tenant and his family could make it less
> likely that it is not reasonable ... I would have thought that, for the
> most part, for both limbs of paragraph 7 to be met, culpability to a
> high and clear degree on the part of the tenant [is] required to be
> shown. Moreover, I would have thought that any landlord such as the
> pursuers, being the district council, responsible for housing a
> substantial element of the community, should expect the court to
> reflect hard whether or not the circumstances of the case, especially
> the nature and extent of the culpability of the tenant, are such as to
> merit the drastic step of putting the tenant out and "maybe on to the
> street".'

[1] (Unrep.) 24th January 1984, Ayr Sheriff Court, Sheriff Grant.

10.2.5.2 In *Falkirk District Council v Townsley* [1] the defender and his wife had, prior to their residence in the house, been travelling people with 'different attitudes and habits', who found it 'difficult to accustom themselves' to the social requirements of their new living conditions [2]. The house was initially without furniture or beds. They had parenting problems which had led to their children being taken into care. They were inarticulate and had difficulty communicating with strangers. The sheriff held, notwithstanding the nuisance and annoyance that had occurred, that

> 'a further attempt or attempts to house the defender before consigning him and his wife once more to homelessness cannot in my opinion be said to be totally without prospects of success although it is clear that to have good prospects of success such an attempt would have to involve considerable commitment (in probability in the face of setbacks and local opposition) from caring agencies outwith the pursuers' responsibility as well as from the pursuers themselves'.

The refusal to grant the order for possession was upheld on appeal to the sheriff principal.

[1] (Unrep.) 25th October 1985, Falkirk Sheriff Court, Sheriff Principal Taylor.

[2] Gypsies are an ethnic minority in terms of section 3(1) of the Race Relations Act 1976; *Commission for Racial Equality v Dutton* [1989] IRLR 8.

10.2.5.3 It may be unreasonable of the local authority landlord not to offer alternative accommodation where the nuisance or annoyance has a 'community care element' [1]. Just how far a landlord will have to go in involving the 'caring agencies' will remain a matter for the discretion of the sheriff in each individual case. It is to be hoped, however, that a court would be slow to grant decree where social work involvement and the provision of services might prevent recurrence of the offending behaviour. In particular, local authority housing departments are increasingly likely to find themselves under pressure from local residents opposed, in particular, to rehousing of the mentally ill in their communities [2]. Misusers of drugs or alcohol may also be persons in need of community care services [3]. Eviction proceedings may have been brought without the housing department requesting the social work department to assess the tenant's need for such services [4]. Alternatively a community care plan might have previously been in place but have broken down and be in need of review [5]. Prior to local government reorganisation, district council housing departments were not obliged by statute to notify the regional council social work department as to a possible need for assessment [6]. There is, however, considerable government guidance stressing the need for such co-operation and inter-agency working [7]. Local authority landlords have duties to allocate and manage housing required by community care groups, and not merely to act as large-scale private landlords [8]. The management role may involve the need to provide housing welfare services to their tenants, including assistance in settling disputes with tenants or neighbours [9]. The Local Government etc. (Scotland) Act 1994 has resulted in housing and social work responsibilities being unified in a single authority with effect from 1st April 1996. Some councils have merged the housing and social work departments. In any event, the local authority landlord also has the statutory responsibilities previously incumbent upon regional councils in respect of assessment and provision of community care.

[1] See Scottish Office Circular SW7/1994, *Community Care - The Housing Dimension*, paragraph 4.6: 'A person's current accommodation (or lack of it) may have a significant effect on their physical and perhaps social functioning; and therefore housing bodies may need to be consulted at the initial stage on this, and how the person's functioning could be affected by alternative housing'.

[2] Housing providers are specifically guided to 'ensure that housing for community care users is not confined to concentrated housing developments, but is integrated and dispersed throughout the community': SW7/1994, paragraph 5.3.2. See also SW1/1992, *Guidance On Care Programmes For People With A Mental Illness Including Dementia*, paragraph 2.2: 'it is therefore important that housing providers should be involved at an early stage in community care planning and at the client level in the preparation of an individuals care programme ... Potential landlords should be advised, so far as confidentiality will allow, of the person's ability to sustain a tenancy and should also be given details of the care manager so that early notification of any housing related or other problems can be given.' See also *National Schizophrenia Fellowship v Ribble Estates SA and Others* (1993) 25 HLR 476 where a declarator was obtained by a charity that housing the mentally ill in a new hostel in a residential area did not contravene burdens in the title to the property in respect of carrying on any 'dangerous trade or pursuit' which was 'noisy' 'offensive' or of 'nuisance annoyance or danger to ... owners or occupiers of any neighbouring property and which may tend to depreciate the value of the property'.

[3] Social Work (Scotland) Act 1968, section 12(1), (6). See also definition of 'community care' in SW7/1994 Annex 3, and *Govanhill Housing Association v Isobel Mackenzie,* supra, at paragraph 8.15.1.

[4] On local authority duties to assess for community care services, see Social Work (Scotland) Act 1968 (as amended by the National Health Service and Community Care Act 1990), section 12A. On process and content of assessment, see SW11/1991, *Community Care – Assessment and Care Management.*

[5] SW1/1992, paragraph 7.1; SW7/1994, paragraph 5.6: 'Whatever the housing placement, the package of accommodation and services provided should be kept under review, and adjusted as necessary to take account of changes in the tenant's condition and circumstances. Sometimes a change of accommodation, including in some cases a move to a residential or institutional establishment, will be required'.

[6] Although the regional council was obliged to notify the housing department and request information where it appeared to them that the person being assessed had a housing need: 1968 Act, section 12A(3)(b). It is important that such matters are brought to the attention of the sheriff in relation to the question of reasonableness before eviction. The failure of the housing authority to exercise its discretion to request assistance from the social services department has been held not to be 'perverse and unreasonable', and therefore not a ground on which a mentally ill tenant evicted for anti-social behaviour could overturn a finding of intentional homelessness: see *R v Wirral Metropolitan Borough Council, ex parte Bell* (1995) 27 HLR 234.

[7] For example, SW7/1994: paragraphs 1.1.1, 1.2, 1.7.2, 2.10.

[8] SW7/1994, paragraphs 2.6, 5.2 – 5.10.

[9] SW7/1994, paragraph 5.9.

10.2.5.4 The question of the reasonableness of not providing alternative accommodation refers to the individual who has misbehaved. Accordingly, if there are joint tenants and only one of them has been guilty of anti-social conduct, there will be no obligation on the landlord to show that it was reasonable not to offer alternative accommodation to the innocent tenant [1]. This innocence might, however, be a factor relevant to reasonableness in respect of section 48(2) of the 1987 Act. In *Clackmannan DC v Morgan* [2], after being satisfied that the (sole) tenant had been guilty of nuisance and annoyance, the sheriff adjourned the proof in order to enable the landlord to consider making alternative accommodation available to his (innocent) cohabitee and her children. They failed to do so. The sheriff accordingly refused the eviction order sought against the tenant:

> 'I think that it is unstateable to suggest that the homelessness of three young children, consequent upon the granting of decree, with apparently small prospects, without uncertain legal procedures, of rehousing should not be included as part of "all the circumstances" in relation to paragraph 7. Bearing in mind the extent of the nuisance or annoyance found by me and that the nuisance or annoyance wholly or almost wholly relates to the defender's actions rather than those of his dependants, the circumstances in the case that the pursuers are not prepared to consider rehousing the dependants and children of the defender unless forced to do so without at least, for example, considering the merits of a particular application for transfer if made is, in my opinion, in the circumstances, unreasonable, unless there are other relevant factors

which are unknown to me ... The onus is on the pursuers to persuade me that the order they seek is reasonable. The evidence shows that an apparently suitable transfer was almost available; there is no evidence that other suitable transfers have been sought or explored or offered by the pursuers without success, the evidence rather being that the pursuers would not have agreed to any transfer even if apparently suitable.'

Accordingly, the sheriff did not seek to distinguish between the reasonableness test in ground 7 and that in section 48(2) of the 1987 Act. In any event, it is likely that part of the burden on the landlord will be to produce evidence to show why it would not be reasonable to rehouse the innocent occupants.

[1] *City of Glasgow District Council v Brown* 1988 SCLR 433 (Sheriff Gordon) and 679 (Sheriff Principal MacLeod).

[2] (Unrep.) 22nd October 1991, Alloa Sheriff Court; Sheriff Younger.

10.3 *'Ground 8: The tenant of the house (or any one of joint tenants) or any person residing or lodging with him or any sub tenant of his has been guilty of conduct in or in the vicinity of the house which is a nuisance or annoyance and in the opinion of the landlord it is appropriate in the circumstances to require the tenant to move to other accommodation.'*

Ground 8 is a request for a compulsory transfer of the anti-social tenant to new accommodation. There are two differences from ground 7: the ground is mandatory, but the landlord is offering alternative accommodation [1]. It is appropriate where the particular living conditions of the tenant have caused or materially contributed to the nuisance [2] and it is therefore thought not likely to occur in alternative accommodation. It may also be appropriate for use in less serious conduct cases as an alternative to outright eviction.

[1] Note also, however, that the sheriff is not entitled in terms of the 1987 Act to adjourn the case: see paragraph 8.15.2 above.

[2] For example, a teenager living in a block of flats otherwise mainly tenanted by elderly people.

10.3.1 The landlord has to show that the transfer is appropriate, but the reasonableness test of section 48(2) of the 1987 Act does not apply to ground 8. If made out, the sheriff has no option but to grant the order for possession.

10.3.2 The alternative accommodation must be suitable [1]. Accommodation will be suitable if it is a secure, assured or protected tenancy, and is reasonably suitable to the needs of the tenant and his family [2]. The onus is on the landlord to show this [3]. However, if the landlord makes a written offer of accommodation which he considers suitable, if the tenant rejects the offer then he will have to show that he did not act unreasonably in so doing [4]. In broad terms, this means considering the proximity of the house to the tenant's workplace, the size and character of the new house relative to the old, terms of the new tenancy and any special needs of the tenant and his family [5]. The landlord must show that the accommodation is available at the date of the proof. Accordingly, the ground will not be satisfied if a tenant has already refused an offer of accommodation which at proof is no longer available [6]. There do not appear to have been any reported decisions in Scotland in relation to the use of ground 8.

[1] 1987 Act, section 48(3).

[2] Schedule 3, Part II, paragraph 1: accordingly it does not have to be accommodation belonging to the pursuer.

[3] *Nevile v Hardy* [1921] 1 Ch 404.

[4] 1987 Act, Schedule 3, Part II, paragraph 3.

[5] These conditions have been considered in various cases: see PQ Watchman (1991), *Housing (Scotland) Act 1987*, Greens, pages 455–6 and Paton and Cameron (1967), *Landlord and Tenant*, Greens, pages 574–6. See also, for example, *Dawncar Investments v Plews* (1993) 25 HLR 639, CA, where the trial judge visited both old and new houses, before refusing the order for possession. The house was not suitable as regards character because of 'noise, traffic, heavy lorries, proximity of railway lines, general roughness of the area and of the inhabitants.'

[6] *Kimpson v Markham* [1921] 2 KB 157.

10.3.3 It is not competent for the sheriff to grant decree in terms of ground 8 where the landlord has sought only to establish ground 7. If the sheriff is not minded to grant decree in terms of ground 7 and the landlord will not agree to make alternative accommodation available, the sheriff has no option but to dismiss the action [1].

[1] See *Clackmannan District Council v Morgan*, supra at paragraph 10.2.5.4.

10.4 Other Grounds for Recovery of Possession of Secure Tenancies

The specific conduct at which grounds 2, 3, and 4 are directed may also constitute nuisance and annoyance within the meaning relevant to ground 7. The advantage to the landlord of using these specific grounds, where appropriate, is that there is no requirement relating to the reasonableness of not offering alternative accommodation. A single court action can seek recovery of possession on these grounds as well as grounds 1 and 7.

10.4.1 *'Ground 2: The tenant (or any one of joint tenants) or any person residing or lodging with him or any sub-tenant of his has been convicted of using the house or allowing it to be used for immoral or illegal purposes.'*

There must be a *conviction* for a criminal offence [1]. This must relate to *use* of the house, and not just the conduct of the tenant *in* the house; for example, using the premises for receiving stolen goods [2]. The house must have been put to an improper use to carry out an unlawful purpose. It is not enough that there has been just an isolated illegal act in carrying out an otherwise lawful purpose [3]. A conviction for the possession of drugs in the house is thus not covered by ground 2. It may well also not be covered by ground 7: it does not necessarily follow that private use of drugs outwith the sight of neighbours constitutes a nuisance or annoyance. In *Scottish Homes v David McCabe* [4] the pursuers sought recovery on the grounds that the defender had been convicted of possession of cannabis resin with intent to supply. Although the ground was made out – the tenant apparently intending to supply the drugs from the house – the sheriff refused the order as unreasonable. He found that the offence had not been repeated, and that the consumption of the cannabis had been confined to a small group of musicians. It is not essential that the charge or conviction in the criminal prosecution should expressly refer to the house. However, the connection between the use of the house and the conviction should be averred and proved [5].

[1] *Frederick Platts Co. Ltd. v Grigor* (1950) 66 (1) TLR 859.

[2] *Schneiders and Sons Ltd. v Abrahams* [1925] 1 KB 301; *Abrahams v Wilson* [1971] 2 QB 88.

[3] So selling alcohol from licensed premises, but out of hours, is insufficient to establish the ground: *Waller and Sons v Thomas* [1921] 1 KB 541. On the other hand, an isolated illegal act for an unlawful purpose will suffice: *Abrahams v Wilson*, supra; *Sweet v Parsley* [1970] AC 132 (the purpose of the use of premises must be other than merely casual or fortuitous); *Schneiders and Sons Ltd v Abrahams*, supra at 306: 'it is necessary to show that the tenant has taken advantage of his tenancy of the premises and of the opportunity they afford for committing the offence.'

[4] (Unrep.) Glasgow Sheriff Court, Sheriff Evans, Glasgow *Evening Times,* 27th May 1994.

[5] *Abrahams v Wilson*, supra.

10.4.2 'Ground 3: The condition of the house or of any of the common parts has deteriorated owing to acts of waste by, or the neglect or default of, the tenant (or any one of joint tenants) or any person residing or lodging with him or any sub-tenant of his; and in the case of waste by, or the neglect or default of, a person lodging with the tenant or by a sub tenant of his, the tenant has not, before the making of the order in question, taken such steps as he ought reasonably to have taken for the removal of the lodger or sub-tenant. In this paragraph "the common parts" means any part of a building containing the house and any other premises which the tenant is entitled under the terms of the tenancy to use in common with the occupiers of other houses.'

10.4.2.1 To establish that the condition of the house or common parts has deteriorated it is necessary to show that there has been at least some physical damage to the structure or fabric of the building. For example, in *Thomson v Ford* [1], the deterioration was a slight bulging of the floor and the ceiling below it. The fact that the tenant has a lack of housekeeping skills will be insufficient if there is no evidence of any actual deterioration [2]. The onus will be on the tenant to show, if s/he can, that the deterioration or dilapidation was due to 'fair wear and tear' and nothing else [3].

[1] (1945) 62 Sh. Ct. Rep. 60.

[2] *Maciver v Struthers* 1924 SLT (Sh Ct) 15.

[3] *Brown v Davies* [1958] 1 QB 117, CA at 127 *per* Lord Evershed MR.

10.4.2.2 Acts of waste or default have been held to include overloading the floors of the house [1], making structural alterations to the house [2], failing to keep the house properly aired and fired [3], or failing to maintain a garden where this is a condition of the tenancy [4].

[1]   *Thomson v Ford*, supra.

[2]   *Marsden v Heyes* [1927] 2 KB 1.

[3]   *Lowe v Lendrum* (1950) 159 EG 423 – although this may in any event be an implied condition of the tenancy and actionable under ground 1.

[4]   *Holloway v Povey* (1984) 15 HLR 104 – even although the garden had been neglected for four years prior to the defender becoming responsible for it. The landlord may of course retain responsibility for maintenance of common ground let with the house – 1987 Act, Schedule 10 and section 338.

10.4.2.3   There must be a causal connection between the acts of waste or neglect and the deterioration of the house or common parts [1].

[1]   *Maciver v Struthers*, supra.

10.4.2.4   The acts of waste or neglect must have been carried out by the tenant, joint tenant, sub-tenant or lodger. There do not appear to be any reported decisions on the question of what a tenant might reasonably do to remove a sub-tenant or lodger. However, the test is not whether a tenant has acted reasonably in evicting his sub-tenant or lodger, but whether he has taken reasonable steps to do so before the order for his own eviction is made. The onus is on the landlord to show what these reasonable steps might be.

10.4.3   'Ground 4: The condition of any furniture provided for use under the tenancy, or for use in any of the common parts (within the meaning given in paragraph 3), has deteriorated owing to ill-treatment by the tenant (or any one of joint tenants) or any person residing or lodging with him or any sub-tenant of his; and in the case of ill-treatment by a person lodging with a tenant or a sub-tenant of his the tenant has not, before the making of the order in question, taken such steps as he ought reasonably to have taken for the removal of the lodger or sub-tenant.'

This ground differs from ground 3 only in that it relates to deterioration of the furniture in the house rather than the house itself. The question of what constitutes 'furniture' has been considered by the English courts. It has been held that the word has a statutory meaning regardless of the terms of the lease and does not include items so fixed to the fabric of the building that appreciable damage would be caused in removing them [1]. It has, however, been held to include fitted cupboards or wardrobes [2], crockery and kitchen utensils [3], linoleum [4], the cooker [5] but not water heaters or panel fires [6]. Failure of the tenant to prevent children causing damage to the furniture and fittings leading to homelessness has been held to justify a finding of intentional homelessness [7].

[1] *Palser v Grinling, Property Holding Co Ltd v Mischeff* [1948] AC 291, HL.

[2] *Gray v Fidler* [1943] KB 694.

[3] *Maddox Properties v Klass* [1946] 1 All ER 487.

[4] *Wilkes v Goodwin* [1923] 2 KB 86.

[5] *New London Properties v Barabas* [1945] EGD 256; *Roppel v Bennett* [1949] 1 KB 115.

[6] *R v Blackpool Rent Tribunal, ex parte Ashton* [1948] 2 KB 277. Although see *R v Hampstead and St Pancras Furnished Houses Rent Tribunal, ex parte Ascot Lodge Ltd* [1947] KB 973.

[7] *R v Rochester upon Medway City Council, ex parte Williams* [1994] EGCS 35.

11 RECOVERY OF POSSESSION: GROUNDS FOR RECOVERY OF POSSESSION OF ASSURED AND PROTECTED TENANCIES

Although the procedure for recovery of possession of assured and protected tenancies differs from that for secure tenancies, the grounds for recovery are very similar, as least as regards nuisance and annoyance caused by the tenant.

11.1 Assured Tenancies

The grounds for recovery of assured tenancies are contained in Schedule 5 to the Housing (Scotland) Act 1988. With a few notable differences, they mirror the grounds for recovery of secure tenancies in relation to anti-social behaviour [1].

[1] This text does not deal with the specialities to be found with short assured tenancies under section 32 of the 1988 Act. See Robson, *Residential Tenancies* at page 99. If a short assured tenancy has been properly created, then at the expiry of the lease, the tenant has no security of tenure. Accordingly, recovery of possession requires no allegation or establishment of neighbour nuisance.

11.1.1 *'Ground 9: Suitable alternative accommodation is available for the tenant or will be available for him when the order for possession takes effect.'*

This ground mirrors ground 8 in the 1987 Act – the compulsory management transfer. There is, however, no requirement to prove any anti-social conduct on the part of the tenant. Accordingly, the only question that arises is as to the suitability of the alternative accommodation [1]. Also, unlike ground 8 of the 1987 Act, it is a discretionary ground: reasonableness must still be proved.

[1] 1988 Act, Schedule 5, Part III, and see paragraph 10.3.2 above.

11.1.2 *'Ground 13: Any obligation of the tenancy (other than one related to the payment of rent) has been broken or not performed.'*

See paragraphs 10.1 *et seq.* above.

11.1.3 *'Ground 14: The condition of the house or of any of the common parts has deteriorated owing to acts of waste by, or the neglect or default*

of, the tenant or any one of joint tenants or any person residing or lodging with him or any sub-tenant of his; and, in the case of acts of waste by, or the neglect or default of, a person lodging with a tenant or a sub-tenant of his, the tenant has not, before the making of the order in question, taken such steps as he ought reasonably to have taken for the removal of the lodger or sub-tenant.'

See paragraphs 10.4.2 *et seq.* above.

11.1.4 *'Ground 15: The tenant or any other person residing or lodging with him in the house has been guilty of conduct in or in the vicinity of the house which is a nuisance or annoyance or has been convicted of using the house or allowing the house to be used for immoral or illegal purposes.'*

This ground mirrors and is an amalgam of grounds 2 and 7 of the 1987 Act. It is more helpful to the landlord, however. There is no requirement that he prove that it is reasonable not to offer alternative accommodation to the tenant. A small private landlord may not have such property available [1].

[1] Alternatively, where the landlord is a large housing association, for example, the failure to offer alternative accommodation would be highly material to the question of the reasonableness of granting decree in terms of the 1988 Act, section 18(4).

11.1.5 *'Ground 16: The condition of any furniture provided for use under the tenancy has deteriorated owing to ill-treatment by the tenant or any other person residing or lodging with him in the house and, in the case of ill-treatment by a person lodging with the tenant or by a sub-tenant of his, the tenant has not taken such steps as he ought reasonably to have taken for the removal of the lodger or sub-tenant.'*

See paragraph 10.4.3 above.

11.2 Protected Tenancies

The grounds for recovery of possession of protected tenancies are to be found in section 11 and Schedule 2 to the Rent (Scotland) Act 1984. There are few significant differences from the considerations already referred to in relation to secure and assured tenancies. The grounds are therefore narrated largely for completeness.

11.2.1 *Case 1:* **'*Where any rent lawfully due from the tenant has not been paid, or any obligation of the protected or statutory tenancy which arises under this Act, or –***

(a) in the case of a protected tenancy, any other obligation of the tenancy, in so far as it is consistent with the provisions of Part II of this Act, or

(b) in the case of a statutory tenancy, any other obligation of the previous protected tenancy which is applicable to the statutory tenancy, has been broken or not performed ...'.

See paragraphs 10.1 *et seq.* above.

11.2.2 *Case 2:* **'*Where the tenant or any person residing or lodging with him or any sub-tenant of his has been guilty of conduct which is a nuisance or annoyance to adjoining occupiers, or has been convicted of using the dwelling-house or allowing the dwelling-house to be used for immoral or illegal purposes.'***

The considerations are largely those relevant in connection with paragraphs 10.2 *et seq.* and 10.4.1 above. The expression 'adjoining occupiers' has, however, been considered in the case law. In *Knapp v Swanson* [1], for example, tenants allegedly causing nuisance and annoyance in one room of a house were held not to be 'adjoining occupiers' of other tenants in the same building. In *Cobstone Investments v Maxim* [2], however, the tenant was accused of verbal abuse and obscene language to tenants in the next door building. The two buildings shared common parts and entrance, but there was no physical contact between them. Following a review of the case law, it was held that it was not correct to define 'adjoining' as meaning 'contiguous' because 'one meaning of the word is "neighbouring" and all that the context seems to require is that the premises of the adjoining occupiers should be near enough to be affected by the tenant's conduct.' Accordingly, the court refused to apply a restrictive interpretation to the expression [3]. Nuisance and annoyance towards the landlord as such (i.e. where s/he is not also a neighbour) will not be caught by this section [4].

[1] (1945) 89 Sol Jo 20.

[2] (1984) 15 HLR 113 (CA).

123

[3] Contrast with paragraph 10.2.4 et seq. above.

[4] *Liffen v France* (1952) 102 L Jo 583.

11.2.3 *Case 3: 'Where the condition of the dwelling-house has, in the opinion of the court, deteriorated owing to acts of waste by, or the neglect or default of, the tenant or any person residing or lodging with him or any sub-tenant of his and, in the case of any act of waste by, or the neglect of, a person lodging with the tenant or a sub-tenant of his, where the court is satisfied that the tenant has not, before the making of the order in question, taken such steps as he ought reasonably to have taken for the removal of the lodger or sub-tenant, as the case may be.'*

See paragraphs 10.4.2 *et seq.* above.

11.2.4 *Case 4: 'Where the condition of any furniture provided for use under the tenancy has, in the opinion of the court, deteriorated owing to ill-treatment by the tenant or any person residing or lodging with him or any sub-tenant of his and, in the case of any ill-treatment by a person lodging with the tenant or a sub-tenant of his, where the court is satisfied that the tenant has not, before the making of the order in question, taken such steps as he ought reasonably to have taken for the removal of the lodger or sub-tenant, as the case may be.'*

See paragraph 10.4.3 above.

11.2.5 *Section 11(1)(a) and Schedule 2, Part IV: '... the court is satisfied that suitable alternative accommodation is available for the tenant or will be available for him when the order in question takes effect ...'*

See paragraphs 11.1.3 and 10.3 *et seq.* above.

12 REASONABLENESS

In most anti-social eviction cases, even where the landlord has proved that a ground for eviction has been established, the sheriff still has a discretion to decide whether the order be granted. A very wide range of circumstances have been considered to be relevant to this discretion, although the sheriff's determination of the question is usually unchallengeable.

12.1 In the case of secure, assured and protected tenancies [1], the sheriff may not make an order for recovery of possession on one of the discretionary grounds unless he is satisfied that it is reasonable to do so. This discretion to refuse an order for possession even where the landlord has made out the case for it being granted has been called the 'overriding equity' [2] and 'the ultimate test of reasonableness' [3]. The court has a 'very wide discretion to take into account all the circumstances at the date of the hearing that may affect the interest of the landlord or tenant including financial hardship to the tenant, the conduct of the parties, and the interest of the public' [4].

[1] Section 48(2)(a) of the 1987 Act (secure), section 11(1) of the 1984 Act (protected) and section 18(4) of the 1988 Act (assured) – the considerations and thus the law are identical in all these types of tenancy.

[2] *Kemp v Ballachulish Estate Company* 1933 SC 478.

[3] *City of Glasgow District Council v Brown* 1988 SCLR 679 at 681 *per* Sheriff Principal MacLeod.

[4] *Falkirk District Council v McLay* 1991 SCLR 895 *per* Sheriff Stein at 897 (approving cases cited in Paton and Cameron, *Landlord and Tenant* (Greens 1967) at pages 571–2; *Cumming v Danson* [1942] 2 All ER 653 at 655.

12.2 The burden of proof is on the landlord to show that it is reasonable to make the order [1]. This burden may in practice rapidly shift to the defender [2]. The pursuer need only make out a prima facie case on reasonableness to require the tenant to show why it is not reasonable for the order to be granted [3]. Unsurprisingly, there is in practice a divergence of views from sheriff to sheriff as to what will be considered 'reasonable'. This is particularly significant given that an appeal court will be very slow to overturn the sheriff's judgment on this question [4]. Nevertheless, the court must consider it in a judicial fashion [5], and will not be immune to challenge from the appeal courts where improper considerations are taken into account or relevant matters excluded or given insufficient weight [6]. Where more than one ground for eviction has been established, the court may consider the question of reasonableness globally and does not have to consider the reasonableness of granting decree under each ground in isolation from the others [7].

[1] *Midlothian District Council v Drummond* 1991 SLT (Sh Ct) 67 at 68 E–F *per* Sheriff Principal O'Brien; *Renfrew District Council v Inglis* 1991 SLT (Sh Ct) 83 *per* Sheriff Principal Hay at 85 B–C.

[2] For example, there is a presumption that deceitful applications for housing should be discouraged: *Link Housing Association v Spence* (unrep.) 12th June 1993, Edinburgh Sheriff Court, Sheriff Scott; *Rushcliffe Borough Council v Watson* (1991) 24 HLR 124, CA approved in *Govanhill Housing Association v McKibbens and Malley* (unrep.) 25th April 1994, Glasgow Sheriff Court, Sheriff Evans.

[3] *City of Glasgow District Council v Erhaiganoma* 1993 SCLR 592.

[4] *Cresswell v Hodgson* [1951] 2 KB 92; *Grandison v Mackay* 1919 1 SLT 95.

[5] *Chiverton v Ede* [1921] 2 KB 30.

[6] See e.g. *Woking Borough Council v Bistram* (1995) 27 HLR 1; *Sheffield City Council v Jepson* (1993) 25 HLR 299, CA; *London Borough of Barking and Dagenham v Hyatt and Hyatt* (1992) 24 HLR 406.

[7] *Glenrothes Development Corporation v Graham* (unrep.) 14th December 1994, Kirkcaldy Sheriff Court, Sheriff Patrick.

12.3   Where there is a deliberate breach of a tenancy agreement and an intention to continue with the breach, it will only be in very special cases that the court will refuse possession [1].   There may be circumstances in which the court can find no basis to find that the landlord has failed to prove that it is reasonable to grant the order [2]. If the tenant wishes to show that it is not reasonable to grant the order where there is a continuing breach, then the reasons for this must be considered at the date of the hearing. In *Green v Sheffield City Council* [3], the tenant wished to keep a dog in breach of his tenancy. He argued that when he had first got the dog the council had agreed to his having it because it gave his wife a feeling of protection against the Yorkshire Ripper. As Dillon J put it, there were two things to consider: first that the Yorkshire Ripper:

> 'has happily been arrested and tried long since, and is not a current danger. The second, less happily, is that Mr Green's marriage has ended in divorce and therefore he no longer has a wife who needs protection'.

The Court of Appeal accordingly refused to overturn the order for possession. In any event, an unexplained failure to attempt to remedy the breach when faced with legal action will attract little sympathy from the court [4].

[1] *Bell London and Provincial Properties Ltd v Reuben* [1947] KB 157.

[2] *Sheffield City Council v Jepson*, supra, where 'the condition itself was necessary ... for the well being of the tenants of the block. The breach was deliberate and persisted in after repeated requests that it cease. The fact of the making of complaints proved that the presence of the dog was affecting other tenants. There is no principle that the council can only prove such a breach of such a condition as will justify the making of an order if it proves also that the forbidden dog has shown itself to have been the direct cause of specific consequences constituting nuisance.'

[3] (1994) 26 HLR 349.

[4] In *Holloway v Povey* (1984) 15 HLR 104, the tenant had failed to maintain the garden of the property. Notwithstanding repeated letters and the court action, and the fact that he had spent over £200 on gardening equipment, he still had made no effort to attend to the garden by the time of the proof.

12.4 The role of the tenant in the breach and the question of whether the incident is an isolated one may make it unreasonable to make an order for recovery, even where the behaviour is extreme. In *Wandsworth London Borough Council v Hargreaves* [1] the lease prohibited the tenant from permitting anything to be done in the premises which might increase the risk of fire, and required him to ensure that he and his visitors to the house did not use the premises in any manner which would cause discomfort, inconvenience, nuisance or annoyance to others. Guests of the tenant subsequently used the flat for making petrol bombs, and in throwing one of the bombs out of the window, set the flat on fire causing serious damage. Nevertheless the order was refused. The judge at proof found that the tenant had not 'permitted' anything to be done to increase fire risk, as he did not know that his guests were doing this [2]. There had been no other incidents since, and the tenant had been allowed back into the flat after repairs. Nevertheless, the case seems exceptional.

[1] (1995) 27 HLR 142.

[2] The Court of Appeal considered this improbable, as the tenant was in the room at the time, and although admittedly drunk, was not incapably so. Nevertheless, the customary reluctance to overturn the judge at first instance prevailed.

12.5 The questions of the length of the tenant's tenancy, and the differing standards that different occupiers may reasonably have, were considered in *Dundee District Council v Heggie* [1]:

> 'What concerns me in this case is that the pursuers appeared to have left almost completely out of account the fact that the Heggies have been tenants of the pursuers and their predecessors, Dundee Corporation, for a period of some 20 years. During that period, so far as the evidence showed, there was only one previous complaint against them, and that was over 15 years ago. The long period of trouble-free tenancy is, in my opinion, a significant factor in determining whether it is reasonable that the pursuers should be required to make other accommodation available to the defender or reasonable that the pursuers should obtain decree for recovery ... it should have occurred to the pursuers that there was a strong possibility that the problem in the present case was, to some extent anyway, explained by the fact that the Heggie's previous neighbours may have had different standards ... and were more tolerant ... If the pursuers had properly applied their minds to this aspect of the case they should in my opinion have given very serious consideration to the possibility of offering the Heggies alternative accommodation. I had the clear impression that the possibility of such an offer had simply been rejected by the pursuers on the basis of complaints made since the Heggies moved to Fullarton Street, with no consideration at all having been given to their previous history.'

[1] (Unrep.) 14th January 1991, Dundee Sheriff Court, Sheriff Stewart (decision upheld before Sheriff Principal Maguire, 14th August 1991).

12.6 It is a factor in reasonableness that if an order for recovery of possession is made, the tenant and his family are likely to be ineligible for permanent rehousing by any local authority [1]. This may create a heavy onus for the pursuers, particularly where there are children involved. In *Clackmannan District Council v Morgan* supra at paragraph 10.2.5.4, the sheriff held that eviction would have:

> 'Draconian consequences for the defender's cohabitee and young children ... being not only that the defender's dependants will lose their present home but also ... that no transfer of tenancy will be considered for them and ... they will become ineligible for rehousing by the pursuers even in their own right ... I consider that a reasonable man would consider it unreasonable to make the order sought ... unless all other possible options to the making of the order sought had been exhausted.'

There has also been said to be a public interest in keeping family units together where eviction might lead to separation of parent from child [2].

[1] Where a tenant has by his anti-social conduct had a decree for eviction pass against him, there is likely to be a presumption that he has made himself 'intentionally homeless' in terms of the 1987 Act, section 26(1). Spouses and cohabitees may be found responsible for the conduct of their partners, parents for the conduct of their children, and tenants for the conduct of non-family members of their household: the key question is whether the family member has acquiesced in the acts or omission which led to homelessness. See cases cited at P.Q. Watchman (1991), *Housing (Scotland) Act 1987* (annotated) Greens 1991, pages 60–62. See in particular *Stewart v Monklands District Council* 1987 SLT 630; *Lewis v North Devon District Council* [1981] 1 All ER 27; *R v Swansea City Council, ex parte Thomas* (1983) 8 HLR 64.

[2] *Rushcliffe Borough Council v Watson* (1991) 24 HLR 124, CA.

12.7 It may have a bearing on reasonableness that the tenant has established, and intends to exercise, a right to buy the property [1].

[1] *London Borough of Enfield v McKeon* (1986) 18 HLR 330. It appears, however, that the government intends to prevent council tenants against whom 'anti-social' eviction proceedings have been commenced from exercising the right to buy (*The Scotsman*, 12th October 1995). Such a response presupposes that the tenant is 'guilty' before any allegation of nuisance has been proved in court.

12.8 While acknowledging that there will be no closed list of factors that will be taken into account by the sheriff in assessing reasonableness, it is submitted that the following (which are not listed in any particular order) should be taken into account:

- seriousness of the conduct
- frequency of the conduct
- length of time over which conduct has occurred
- nature of the conduct complained of
- where the conduct was by a person other than the defender, the steps that have been taken to control the offender
- the length of the tenancy and any previous problems
- conduct of the other neighbours
- effect of behaviour on neighbours
- effect of behaviour on landlord's ability to let adjoining property
- whether the conduct complained of has abated at the time of the hearing
- efforts made by the landlord to involve other agencies: e.g. police, social work department, environmental health
- effect of eviction on any innocent members of the household, particularly dependent children

- other steps taken or considered by the landlord to deal with the problem by non-legal means: e.g. mediation, insulation against noise nuisance, interdict [1]
- whether the conduct was intentional or had some other cause: e.g. the defender's mental health problems

[1] The landlords failure to communicate the complaints about her son to the tenant, failure to attempt any round table discussion, and failure to implement recognised procedures for dealing with neighbour nuisance, were all criticised in *Dundee District Council v Anderson* (unrep.) 8th September 1993, Dundee Sheriff Court, Sheriff MacFarlane.

12.9 The issue of the tenant's allegedly anti-social conduct during a previous tenancy with the same landlord has been held to be irrelevant to the question of reasonableness [1].

[1] *Dundee District Council v Rice* (unrep.) 8th October 1991, Dundee Sheriff Court, Sheriff Raeburn.

12.10 The propriety of the council's policy in refusing to waive a prohibition in the lease has been held to be an improper consideration in the assessment of reasonableness. In *London Borough of Barking v Hyatt and Hyatt* [1], the tenants parked a caravan outside their house in breach of an express prohibition. It was the council's policy never to waive the restriction. The judge was 'not satisfied that individual consideration was ever given to the circumstances of these tenants ... it is not sufficient that no proper consideration is given'. This was held on appeal to be a misdirection, and a new trial ordered. The judge was not entitled to embark upon a judicial review of the council's policy [2].

[1] (1992) 24 HLR 406.

[2] And see *R v London Borough of Barnett, ex parte Gumbridge* (1992) 24 HLR 433. See, however, *Wandsworth London Borough Council v Winder* [1985] AC 461 where an action for possession for non-payment of rent was successfully defended on the basis that the council's policy in increasing the rent was unlawful. See also *City of Aberdeen District Council v Christie* 1983 SLT (Sh Ct) 57 distinguishing *Edinburgh District Council v Parnell* 1980 SLT (Sh Ct) 11.

13. EVIDENCE

Whether the landlord is seeking interdict, eviction, lawburrows or some other remedy, the relevant facts must first be established according to the rules of evidence. A clear appraisal of the quality and quantity of evidence is required before commencing legal action.

A complaint of landlords sometimes heard is that their lawyers tell them the evidence available is insufficient to raise a court action where it is felt that the case could not be clearer [1]. The landlord usually must accept the advice of the lawyer. Equally, tenant defenders may be advised by their lawyers that no defence is possible because the pursuer's case is too strong. The tenant feels s/he must accept the lawyer's opinion. The law of evidence is often arcane and full of fine distinctions. It uses jargon, some of which has entered common speech, but no better understood for all that. This chapter is aimed at both lawyers and non-lawyers. For the lawyer it will revise the principal concepts with particular reference to legal actions based on neighbour nuisance. For the non-lawyer it attempts to make clearer the legal concepts involved in evidence. This chapter is necessarily a simplified summary [2].

[1] See, for example, Clapham et al. (1995), paragraph 11.57.

[2] Seek further information from one of the standard texts in this area: Civil Evidence (Scotland) Act 1988, annotated with commentary by Field; *Stair Memorial Encyclopaedia*, Volume 10; MacPhail (1987), *Evidence* (Revised Research Paper), Law Society of Scotland; Field (1988), *The Law of Evidence in Scotland*, Greens (new edition forthcoming (1997) by Field and Rait); Walker and Walker (1964), *Law of Evidence in Scotland*, Hodge; Wilkinson (1986), *The Scottish Law of Evidence*, Butterworths/Law Society of Scotland; Cross and Tapper (1985), *Cross on Evidence*; Dickson (3rd ed, 1887) *A Treatise on the Law of Evidence in Scotland*, Greens.

13.1 In summary, for the landlord to obtain decree for eviction [1], or for interdict [2] s/he must discharge the burden of proof. To do this, the landlord must adduce sufficient relevant and credible evidence of such weight as to satisfy the court on the balance of probabilities that the grounds for eviction or interdict have been made out. Each of these concepts is now explored.

[1] See Chapters 9–12.

[2] See Chapter 4. Note that when seeking interim interdict, no evidence need be led; the pursuer needs to satisfy the court that s/he has a prima facie (at first sight) case and that the balance of convenience favours the granting of interim interdict.

13.2 In simple terms, the burden (or onus) of proof is on the pursuer landlord. That is, it is for the pursuer to make out his case to the required standard since s/he is asserting breach of the tenancy conditions or nuisance etc. [1]. On each and every issue in a case, there is a burden of proof which attaches to one or other of the parties and this remains constant throughout the case [2]. A party may fail to meet the burden of proof because the evidence is insufficient [3] in law or fails to prove the issue at hand on the balance of probabilities [4] (perhaps because the court may prefer the evidence of the other party). The party bearing the burden of proof must prove all material facts that are not admitted [5]. There is no need to prove facts which are judicially noted [6] or facts which are res judicata [7]. The party seeking to discharge the burden of proof may be assisted by legal presumptions of fact or law [8].

[1] More precisely, however, there is not one but two burdens of proof: the persuasive burden and the evidential burden. In civil cases, such as eviction or interdict, the distinction between these two burdens is usually of little significance as the party bearing the persuasive burden will normally bear also the evidential burden. See further, MacPhail, *Law of Evidence*, Chapter 22; Field (1988), Chapter 2; Wilkinson (1986), Chapter 12.

[2] Field (1988) at paragraph 2.2; see Wilkinson at page 181 for a discussion of the sense in which the burden of proof may be said to shift during a case.

[3] See paragraph 13.5 below.

[4] I.e. the standard of proof. See paragraph 13.3 below.

[5] Admitted in the written pleadings, in a joint minute of admissions, by oral admission before the court or by the party in his/her evidence. In some circumstances, a party may be held to have impliedly admitted a particular fact in his/her pleadings. See MacPhail, *Sheriff Court Practice*, paragraphs 9.20 *et seq.*

[6] That is, which the law assumes are within the knowledge of the court: for example drinking, singing, and shouting are normal at Hogmanay. See Field (1988), Chapter 4.

[7] I.e. facts already decided in a previous court case – e.g. that the tenant was guilty of conduct leading to a conviction for breach of the peace.

[8] For which see generally Field (1988), Chapter 3; Wilkinson at pages 192 *et seq.*

13.2.1 There is a general presumption of law in favour of innocence and freedom from fault whether in a moral or legal sense which applies to both criminal and civil cases [1]. There is a presumption in favour of regularity and validity both in formal transactions and in private transactions [2]. For example, there is a presumption that books kept in the ordinary course of business are accurate and that the ordinary practice of the business has been followed [3] so that where, for example, a landlord pursuer lodges housing records, the presumption is that the records are accurate. A probative writ is assumed to have been validly executed [4]. However, no such presumption attaches to documents which are merely holograph or adopted as holograph which require to be proved if their validity is challenged [5]. It should be noted that such presumptions are rebuttable, that is, the presumption can be displaced if evidence is led to show that, for example, the housing records are not in fact accurate. The validity of non-probative documents can be challenged by any means in the court action itself.

[1] *Odiosa et inhonesta non sunt in lege praesumenda*; Wilkinson at page 196. The effect of this presumption on the standard of proof where an allegation of a criminal nature in a civil case is being made is discussed at paragraph 13.3.1 below. See also *Gibson v NCR Ltd* 1925 SLT 377 and *McClure Naismith Brodie and Macfarlane v Stewart* (1887) 15 R (HL) 1.

[2] *Omnia praesumuntur rite ac solemniter esse acta*. See, for example, *Bain v Assets Co.* (1905) 7 F (HL) 104 at 106: 'every intendment should be made in favour of what has been done as being lawfully and properly done'.

[3] Dickson (3rd ed. 1888) at 114–20; *Guthrie v Stewart* 1926 SC 743; *City of Edinburgh District Council v MacDonald* 1979 SLT (Sh Ct) 58. See also Civil Evidence (Scotland) Act 1988, section 5, relating to evidence of business records.

[4] That is, a formal document which has been drawn up in accordance with formal rules (such as most leases issued by local authorities and housing associations). See Walker and Walker (1964) at 178. Such a document may only be challenged by means of an action of reduction in the Court of Session: *McBeath's Trs. v McBeath* 1935 SC 471.

[5] The legal significance of the phrase 'adopted as holograph' which has been used by many public landlords to formalise the execution of leases, has been removed by the Requirements of Writing Act 1995 in respect of documents signed on or after 1st August 1995.

13.3 Standard of Proof

13.3.1 There are only two standards of proof in Scots law: proof on the balance of probabilities and proof beyond reasonable doubt [1]. Proof on the balance of probabilities is the general rule in civil cases such as for eviction or interdict. In such cases the pursuer must satisfy the court that it is more probable than not that the fact exists or occurred [2]. If the probabilities are evenly balanced, the pursuer will fail [3]. What is being weighed in the balance are not quantities of evidence but the probabilities arising from the acceptable evidence and all the circumstances of the case [4]. Proof beyond all reasonable doubt is the standard usually applicable to criminal cases [5]. In order to qualify as a reasonable doubt, there must be something more than a 'strained or fanciful acceptance of remote possibility' [6]. In some types of civil action, the standard of proof is, however, the higher test of beyond all reasonable doubt: for example, in an action for breach of interdict [7], and contravention of lawburrows [8]. The reason appears to be that the penalty in both types of action includes the possibility of imprisonment.

[1] *Brown v Brown* 1972 SC 123; *Lamb v Lord Advocate* 1976 SC 110; and *Mullan v Anderson* 1993 SLT 835, 1993 SCLR 506, IH (Bench of five judges at 514B, 517B, 524A and 531A). See, generally, MacPhail on *Evidence* paragraph 22.29 *et seq*; *Stair Memorial Encyclopaedia*, Vol. 10, paragraphs 758 *et seq*.

[2] *Simpson v London, Midland and Scottish Railway Co* 1931 SC (HL) 15 at 20, 1931 SLT 170 at 172.

[3] See, for example, *Hendry v Clan Line Steamers Ltd* 1949 SC 320.

[4] MacPhail on *Evidence*, paragraph 22.30.

[5] *Stair Memorial Encyclopaedia*, Vol. 11 at paragraph 759.

[6] *Irving v Minister of Pensions* 1945 SC 21 at 29.

[7] For example, *Gribben v Gribben* 1976 SLT 266.

[8] *Morrow v Neil* 1975 SLT (Sh Ct) 65 at 69. See further Chapter 5, supra.

13.3.2 Where a pursuer alleges the occurrence of a criminal act in the course of a civil case, the standard of proof is on balance of probabilities. The more serious the allegation, however, the higher the degree of probability required [1].

[1] *Sloan v Triplett* 1985 SLT 294 at 297. See also *Hornal v Neuberger Products Ltd* [1957] 1 QB 247 at 258; *B v Kennedy* 1987 SLT 765 at 768; *R v Hampshire County Council, ex parte Ellerton* [1985] 1 WLR 749. Older Scottish authorities took a different view: see, for example, *Cullens Trs v Johnston* (1865) 3 M 935; *Wink v Speirs* (1867) 6 M 77 (fraud); *Arnott v Burt* (1872) 11 M 62 (forgery).

13.4 Classification of Types of Evidence

Evidence may be primary or secondary. Primary evidence is the best form of evidence available to prove an issue (for example, the original lease agreement). Secondary evidence is by definition less than best (for example, a copy of the original lease). The general requirement is that where the best available evidence is not led, a good explanation is required [1]. However,

Evidence

even though secondary evidence is now generally admissible, it may not have sufficient weight to discharge the burden of proof [2]. Thus, a landlord pursuer is best advised to lead the oral evidence of the neighbour who says she saw the anti-social conduct rather than the (hearsay) oral evidence of the housing officer who says the neighbour told her she saw the anti-social behaviour. Similarly the tenant defender may seek to attack the strength of the landlord's case by arguing that available primary evidence has not been led [3].

[1] See Field, paragraph 8.6. This is particularly the case if the best evidence is destroyed whilst in the hands of the party seeking to rely on the copies: *Scottish and Universal Newspapers v Ghersons' Trustees* 1987 SC 27, 1988 SLT 109. This distinction was once encapsulated in what was known as the 'best evidence' rule whereby secondary evidence was generally inadmissible. The position has now been considerably changed not least by the Civil Evidence Scotland Act 1988. Section 2 makes hearsay evidence (a type of secondary evidence) competent (considered further in the next paragraph). Section 6 allows for certified copy documents to be treated as a true copy. Sections 2 and 3 allow statements made and lodged in court to be admissible as evidence of their contents. (As to procedure for admitting such statements, see paragraphs 13.4.3 *et seq*, below.

[2] See, for example, *Stewart v Glasgow Corporation* 1958 SC 28 (failure to produce defective clothes pole) and *McGowan v Belling & Co* 1983 SLT 77 (electric fire) for examples of the importance of producing the best evidence available.

[3] 'While there is no general rule of law that secondary evidence is excluded when primary evidence can be adduced, if a party chooses to rely on secondary evidence when primary evidence is available, the judge of the facts may not be disposed to attach weight to the secondary evidence on the view that it has probably been presented in the hope that it will produce a better impression than the primary evidence would create.' W .J. Lamb, *A Manual of the Law of Evidence in Scotland* (1925), page 256 quoted in *Stair Memorial Encyclopaedia*, Volume 10, paragraph 778.

13.4.1 Hearsay

13.4.1.1 Hearsay evidence is a type of secondary evidence. It is evidence given by a person of what another person heard, or saw, or otherwise perceived with his senses. Hearsay evidence also includes entries in documents made otherwise than by the person giving evidence in court. It includes statements made on a previous occasion by any person including the person giving evidence in court. The traditional rule was that, with various exceptions, hearsay evidence was inadmissible in both civil and criminal proceedings [1].

135

[1] For a lengthy analysis, see MacPhail on *Evidence*, Chapter 19 (written prior to the coming into force of the Civil Evidence (Scotland) Act 1988). Some of the reasons for such inadmissibility are as follows: (a) hearsay evidence cannot be cross-examined; (b) it is evidence not given under oath; (c) it is not best evidence; (d) there are obvious dangers of inaccuracies; (e) the evidence may be concocted. The disadvantages of the rule have been noted as follows: (a) reliable evidence may be excluded; (b) impossibility or expense of adducing admissible direct evidence; (c) disturbance of the natural flow of testimony; (d) complications in defining exceptions to the rule; (e) divergence between evidence admissible in courts on the one hand and in tribunals, inquiries and arbitrations on the other.

13.4.1.2 Hearsay evidence is now admissible in all civil proceedings [1]. Thus in any eviction or interdict action, the court will be entitled to find a case proved on the balance of probabilities based entirely on hearsay evidence [2]. However, merely because the courts are 'entitled' does not mean that they must find the fact proved. It is still for the court to determine whether the evidence is sufficient [3]. The pursuer landlord in a neighbour nuisance eviction case will frequently rely on hearsay evidence of housing officers, professional witnesses and others in situations where the victims of the nuisance claim to have been intimidated or fear reprisals [4].

[1] Section 2(1)(c) of the Civil Evidence (Scotland) Act 1988 provides that 'the court ... if satisfied that any fact has been established by evidence in those proceedings shall be entitled to find that fact proved by the evidence notwithstanding that the evidence is hearsay'. This includes hearsay 'of whatever degree': 1988 Act, section 9. Note also that the use of the word 'solely' in section 2(1)(a) indicates that hearsay may be excluded for some other reason – for example, it is irrelevant.

[2] Which does not need to be corroborated: 1988 Act, section 1. See *Ferguson v S* 1993 SCLR 712 for an example of where a fact was found proved based on hearsay evidence. This means, for example, that it is conceivable that a decree for eviction could be granted based on the hearsay evidence of one housing officer as to nuisance complaints. See, for example, the use of uncorroborated hearsay to establish a crucial fact in *Braedale Garage v Steele* 1995 GWD 35–1798.

[3] See paragraph 13.5 below. The reasons for the previous exclusion of hearsay evidence (noted at 13.4.1.1,n1 above) still have some validity and such factors will influence the weight that will be given by a court to hearsay evidence.

[4] In *Dundee District Council v Janet Westwater* (unrep.) 11th May 1995, Dundee Sheriff Court, Sheriff Eccles, the pursuers led substantial hearsay evidence spoken to by a housing officer and by a trainee solicitor. The sheriff indicated that the hearsay evidence by the housing officer must have some weight but discounted the evidence of the trainee solicitor employed by the pursuer.

13.4.2 Direct and circumstantial evidence are both led in the majority of civil cases. Direct evidence is evidence of a fact in issue which is given by a witness who perceived it with his own senses or which is apparent from the court's inspection of a document or object produced. Circumstantial evidence is indirect evidence of a fact in issue from which the fact in issue may be inferred [1]. Circumstantial evidence alone, if weighty enough, may be sufficient to prove any disputed fact. In very general terms, circumstantial evidence is weaker than direct evidence [2]. There is no rule that circumstantial evidence is inadmissible if direct evidence is available [3]. However, if direct evidence is available and not led without good reason, the evidential value of the circumstantial evidence may be impaired [4].

[1] Walker and Walker, *The Law of Evidence in Scotland* (1964), paragraphs 5, 6, 8–13. For example, Mrs McGinty's evidence that she saw Mrs. McDonald's children set fire to the midden is direct evidence. Mr McGinty's evidence that he saw the children running away from the smouldering remains is circumstantial.

[2] Not least because of the dangers inherent in the court drawing the incorrect inference from the evidence.

[3] Dickson, paragraph 199.

[4] Dickson, paragraphs 108(7) and 199.

13.4.3 Documentary and Real Evidence

13.4.3.1 Documentary evidence includes not only written documents (such as housing records, statements, leases) but also maps, plans, photographs, audio and visual recordings [1]. All such evidence is potentially admissible subject to the rules, conditions and exceptions noted below. Real evidence is a tangible and physical thing (such as a blood sample, clothing, broken door or even a person) from which some significant inference may be drawn [2]. It is normally lodged as a production. In practice, it is submitted, the distinction between real and documentary evidence will have little relevance. Where pertinent real evidence is available, the prudent party to an action will lodge and use such evidence, particularly since such evidence will form direct primary evidence [3]. Real and documentary evidence, once lodged, will require to be spoken to by a witness or agreed by joint minute between the parties [4].

[1] Civil Evidence (Scotland) Act 1988, section 9.

[2] See, for example, Field, paragraph 8.3.

[3] For which see supra at paragraphs 13.4 and 13.4.2. See also Field, paragraph 8.3.

[4] E.g. *Hamilton v HMA* 1980 JC 66.

13.4.3.2 Written statements, precognitions and affidavits

A written statement is simply a statement of a person about a particular fact or facts [1]. It need not be signed, witnessed or sworn. It may be written personally by that person or by another. In a neighbour nuisance case, such statements may typically be letters from complaining neighbours, a statement taken by a housing officer or a statement in the housing records by that housing officer. It includes statements made to a police officer when the maker is only regarded as a witness [2]. By contrast a precognition is a statement which is prepared for the purposes of the court proceedings by one of the parties to those proceedings. It is usually prepared by a solicitor or by specialist precognition agents employed by him. It is usually unsigned and unsworn. Precognitions are inadmissible as evidence [3]. This is because they do not necessarily reflect the true recollections of the witness but are 'filtered through the mind of another' and are usually over-optimistic [4]. An affidavit is a statement sworn to be true (on oath) before a notary public and signed by the notary public and the deponent (the maker of the affidavit).

[1] See 1988 Act, section 9: statement includes any representation (however made or expressed) of fact or opinion but does not include a statement in a precognition.

[2] *Aitchison v Simon* 1976 SLT (Sh Ct) 73 and *Hall v HMA* 1968 SLT 275.

[3] Civil Evidence (Scotland) Act 1988, sections 2, 3 and 9. See *McAvoy v Glasgow District Council* 1993, SLT 859, 1993 SCLR 393 OH, for a more detailed analysis of the difference between a statement and a precognition.

[4] *Kerr v HMA* 1958 JC 14 at 19.

13.4.3.3 Section 2(1)(b) of the Civil Evidence (Scotland) Act 1988 provides that 'a statement made by a person otherwise than in the course of proof shall be admissible as evidence of any matter contained in the statement of which direct oral evidence by that person would be admissible'. The definition of statement is broad [1] and includes any representation of fact or opinion, including affidavits but excluding precognitions [2]. However, for a statement to be admissible, direct oral evidence from the maker of the statement must also be admissible. Thus, if the written pleadings do not contain a record of the matters referred to in the pleadings, or the maker is not a competent witness (for example, s/he is insane), the statements are not admissible.

[1] 1988 Act, section 9.

[2] It is still possible to lodge a precognition in court and confront a witness with its contents with a view to confirming or discrediting his version of events given in oral testimony.

13.4.3.4 Where a written statement is admissible, either the maker of the statement or another person with knowledge of it can give oral evidence to establish it [1]. Alternatively, there is a formal procedure whereby the contents of a statement can be admitted as evidence without oral testimony [2]. Using this last course is unlikely to give the statement much weight, especially if its contents are contradicted by other direct evidence [3].

[1] Simply lodging a written document 'in process' at the court does not give the sheriff the right to take notice of either its existence or its content. What is needed is someone who can both say that the statement is what it bears to be (e.g. a letter of complaint from a neighbour) and speak to the truth of what it contains (e.g. that the tenant did in fact play loud music on the night of 23rd January etc.).

[2] OCR 29.3. This rule is also applicable to summary cause actions: see Act of Sederunt (Sheriff Court Ordinary Cause Rules) 1993 (SI 1993/1956), section 3. (Note that the version of the Rules published by Greens (1995) is incorrect at section 3 where the applicability of OCR 29.3 to summary cause is omitted in error.). A motion must be made to the court for the statement to be received in evidence. The sheriff may admit the statement subject to conditions as he sees fit. The granting of such a motion does not imply that the statement is credible or reliable: see *McVinnie v McVinnie* 1995 SLT (Sh Ct) 81 (Sheriff MacPhail). See also *Lobban v Philip* 1995 SCLR 1104 dissenting from *McVinnie v McVinnie*.

[3] *McVinnie v McVinnie*, supra; *Smith v Alexander Baird Ltd* 1993 SCLR 563.

13.4.3.5 Prior statements made by a witness which are inconsistent with his oral testimony may be put to him in order to challenge his credibility [1]. However, it is not permissible to seek to have that statement taken as evidence itself instead of the witness's evidence: the purpose is to discredit the witness, not to have the statement taken as good evidence [2]. A statement of a witness who has yet to give evidence may not be put to another witness before the maker of the statement has spoken to it [3]. It is thought that for these purposes, an affidavit, despite being sworn before a notary public, will not necessarily carry more weight than an unsworn statement. Affidavits are frequently edited by the notary public, who will in practice usually be involved in the case. Thus their value is tainted.

[1] See for example *Dorona v Caldwell* 1981 SLT (N) 91.

[2] Field, page 213.

[3] *Davis v McGuire* 1995 SLT 755 (thus, in this case necessitating the recall of a witness).

13.4.4 Documents of a 'business or undertaking' can be certified as such by an officer of the business in writing. Those documents may then be received in evidence without being spoken to by a witness [1]. 'Documents' includes computer records [2]. 'Business undertaking' includes any public or statutory undertaking, local authorities and government departments [3]. Copies of original documents can be treated as if they were the originals if authenticated by the person making the copies [4].'Negative facts' of information contained in business records, can be evidenced by an officer of the business or undertaking without the need to produce all the records [5].

[1] Unless the court directs otherwise: Civil Evidence (Scotland) Act 1988, section 5.

[2] 1988 Act, section 9.

[3] 1988 Act, section 9.

[4] 1988 Act, section 6. The documents must be authenticated prior to the proof. If not, they may be found inadmissible: *McIlveney v Donald* 1995 SCLR (N) 802.

[5] 1988 Act, section 7. For example, a witness may give evidence that a particular entry relating to a complaint is not contained in the record, rather than having to get all the records produced and examining each one before concluding that no such entry exists.

13.5 Sufficiency and Weight of Evidence.

Whether the court will find the facts proved sufficient to establish the pursuer's case will depend on its assessment of the sufficiency and weight of evidence adduced. Naturally this is not an exact or scientific process. The court will have regard to such matters as assessment of the credibility and reliability of witnesses; the quality of the evidence (whether the evidence is direct or hearsay, primary or secondary, etc.); to the coherence of the evidence as a whole; and to whether evidence is corroborated [1]. Evidence not relevant to the matters at issue will be excluded [2]. Some of these matters will now be examined in more detail [3].

[1] Even though corroboration is not now a strict requirement in most civil cases: Civil Evidence (Scotland) Act 1988, section 1. See paragraph 13.5.2 below and *Stair Memorial Encyclopaedia*, Vol. 10 at paragraph 774.

[2] See *Dundee District Council v Rice* (unrep.) 8th October 1991, Dundee Sheriff Court (evidence as to conduct of previous tenancy rejected as irrelevant).

[3] For other matters relating to sufficiency and weight of evidence, see Field at paragraph 1.5 and *Stair Memorial Encyclopaedia*, Vol. 10 at paragraph 762 *et seq.*

13.5.1 Reliability and Credibility

Credibility relates to whether the witness is telling the truth as s/he knows it (whether or not the witness is accurate). Reliability relates to the accuracy of the witness's evidence. Thus, a witness who honestly believes that she saw Mike hit John may be credible even though video evidence establishes conclusively that John hit Mike. The witness's evidence, at least on that point, is not reliable. The court will come to a view on the credibility and reliability of witnesses having regard to their general demeanour in court, the manner in which they reply to questions and the extent to which their evidence stands up to cross-examination [1]. The court, as a result, may place great weight on that witness's evidence or, perhaps, no weight at all. The higher courts will be slow to interfere with the assessment of the court where the evidence was led, at least as regards credibility and reliability in civil cases [2].

[1] See Field, Chapter 9 on cross-examination generally. The assessment does not depend on any rule of law but on experience and common sense!

[2] *Thomas v Thomas* 1948 SC (HL) 45 at 54 and *Stair Memorial Encyclopaedia*, Vol. 10, at paragraph 781. See also MacPhail, *Sheriff Court Practice*, paragraphs 18.101 *et seq.*

13.5.2 Corroboration

By corroboration is meant the rule that any essential or material fact must be found proved from more than one source. In civil cases, the requirement of corroboration has been abolished [1]. Thus, an essential fact, such as that the defender held a late-night party during which a television exited the upstairs window could be proved on the evidence of a single neighbour without the need for other corroborative evidence such as a police report, housing officers' evidence or indeed, the remains of the television itself. This is, of course, not to say that any uncorroborated evidence introduced will necessarily succeed in establishing the fact. Where a pursuer is not corroborated on crucial facts, the evaluation and assessment of his evidence requires special care and attention [2]. It is prudent to call any other available corroborative evidence to establish credibility and reliability [3]. Thus, notwithstanding the abolition of the corroboration rule by the 1988 Act, the presence or absence of corroboration remains an important consideration for the court in deciding whether or not a fact has been proved [4].

[1] Civil Evidence (Scotland) Act 1988, section 1. The requirement for corroboration in criminal cases still exists subject to certain statutory exceptions.

[2] *McLaren v Caldwells Paper Mill Co. Ltd* 1973 SLT 158 at 164 and 165.

[3] *Sands v George Waterston & Sons Ltd* 1989 SLT 174, discussed in D. Field, 'Going it Alone', 1989 SLT (News) 216.

[4] See *Morrison v J. Kelly and Sons Ltd* 1970 SC 65 at 80 (which relates to a similar relaxation in the corroboration rule introduced by section 9 of the Law Reform (Miscellaneous Provisions) (Scotland) Act 1968).

13.5.3 Coherence of Evidence [1]

In assessing the weight of evidence, the court will have regard not only to the credibility and reliability of individual witnesses and other evidence but also to the coherence of the evidence as a whole. Where many pieces of evidence indicate the existence of a fact, the weight of the aggregate is very much greater than the weight of each piece taken separately [2]. Failure to call as a witness any available person who is more directly in possession of the truth of any matter than the witnesses who were called to prove it may adversely affect the weight of the evidence led [3]. The failure of a party to lead any evidence at all in rebuttal of the evidence led by his opponent cannot be construed as an admission of the opponent's case [4]. Failure to do so may be dealt with by the court drawing only the most favourable inferences from the opponent's evidence. It is frequently the case in anti social conduct cases that allegations have been made over a considerable period, sometimes as long as ten years. Where there has been a considerable lapse of time between the event being inquired into and the date of the trial or proof, it may be necessary for the court to examine the evidence with special care [5].

[1] See *Stair Memorial Encyclopaedia*, Vol. 10, paragraph 780.

[2] *Lord Advocate and the Clyde Trustees v Lord Blantyre* (1879) 6 R (HL) 72 at 85.

[3] See *Coles v Homer & Tulloh* (1893) 22 R 716 at 732.

[4] *Faddes v M'Neish* 1923 SC 443.

[5] *Rutherford v Harvey & M'Millan* 1954 SLT (Notes) 28; *Dingwall v J. Wharton (Shipping) Ltd* [1961] 2 Lloyd's Rep 213; *McLaren v Caldwells Paper Mill Co Ltd,* supra; *Rafferty v J. & C. M. Smith (Whiteinch) Ltd* 1990 SLT 2 at 5.

13.6 Sources of Evidence

In any case involving allegations of anti-social behaviour, there are likely to be a large number of sources of evidence. A landlord in developing its policies on anti-social behaviour should have regard to the recommendations made on good practice in housing management since, by adopting such practices (including accurate, relevant and timeous record-keeping), it will also be providing a valuable source of evidence for any subsequent court proceedings [1]. Oral evidence or statements or reports or letters [2] from affected neighbours, housing officers, police, environmental health officers and private detectives may be used in evidence. Photographs, video and audio recordings are admissible [3] and often of great value. Reports and oral evidence of professionals such as doctors, social workers, architects, surveyors, psychiatrists may also be relevant in many anti-social behaviour cases. Where one side possesses evidence which may be useful to the other, it may be recovered by court order as discussed in the next paragraph.

[1] See generally Chapter 2, supra.

[2] See paragraph 13.4.3.2, supra.

[3] Civil Evidence (Scotland) Act 1988, section 9.

13.7 Specification of Documents

13.7.1 A party to legal action may need to recover documents from the other side before proof. In practice, the party wishing to do so is most likely to be the tenant [1]. Again, this should be routinely considered by a defender's agents in anti-social eviction and interdict cases. Where a tenant has not been successful in remitting the case to ordinary cause procedure and especially where the landlord has adopted a minimalist approach to pleadings, it will be essential for the tenant to obtain more details of the complaints against him. The documents sought to be recovered must be relevant to the facts as averred in the pleadings [2]. There is no rule that the documents sought to be recovered should themselves be admissible as evidence [3]. Fishing diligences are prohibited: that is where a party is simply hoping to get documents which perhaps will assist his case and which do not pertain to averments in the pleadings of either party [4]. Communications passing between a client and his professional legal adviser are irrecoverable [5]. As a general rule, no party can recover from his opponent material which the opponent has made in preparing his own case [6].   Private documents will be protected from recovery as far as possible and the court may exercise its discretion to refuse recovery if the information can be obtained from other sources which do not involve disclosing private information [7].   Where the documents are sought to be recovered from a government department such as the police, there may be a public interest immunity objection. This is a complex area [8].   In anti-social eviction cases, however, the police will normally be willing to supply an extract of a report of incidents and may afford facilities for the precognition of the police officers concerned.

[1]   The legal process for doing so is known as obtaining commission and diligence for a specification of documents: see Summary Cause Rule 37 and Ordinary Cause Rules, Chapter 28. It is beyond the scope of this work to go into detail on the procedure and the law. The most comprehensive work in this area is McSporran and Young: (1995), *Commission and Diligence*, Greens. See also MacPhail, *Sheriff Court Practice*, Chapter 18; MacPhail on *Evidence*, Chapter 25.

[2]   See generally MacPhail, *Sheriff Court Practice*, Chapter 15.

[3]   *Admiralty v Aberdeen Steam Trawling and Fishing Co. Ltd* 1909 SC 335; *Wheatley v Anderson* 1927 SC 133; *Johnston v South of Scotland Electricity Board* 1968 SLT (Notes) 7.

[4]   See, for example, *Earl of Morton v Fleming* 1921 1 SLT 205.

[5]   See Walker, *Evidence*, page 1414; MacPhail on *Evidence*, paragraphs 18.20 to 18.22.

[6]   *Anderson v St Andrews Ambulance Association* 1942 SC 555.

[7]   Thus, where the landlord is in possession of documents such as letters provided to it by other tenants relating to complaints about the defender, the pursuer landlord may be able to object to their being recovered if it can show that either the documents are not relevant or that the documents are private to that third party and that the information contained within them can be obtained from other sources such as from its own records. See *Science Research Council v Nassé* [1980] AC 1028 *per* Lord Fraser of Tullybelton at 1086.

[8]   See further MacPhail, *Sheriff Court Practice*, paragraphs 4.71 to 4.74.

13.7.2   The specification of documents is sought by means of an incidental application (or motion) to the sheriff who has a discretion as to whether to allow specification in whole or in part [1].   Where the application is granted, documents can be recovered if necessary by means of a commission. providing the court has not only granted the specification of documents but has also granted commission and diligence for their recovery and has appointed a commissioner [2].   It may be necessary to discharge any diet of proof previously fixed to provide time for the documents to be produced which may cause delay.   Again this would be a matter for the discretion of the sheriff. Where the specification of documents is refused by the sheriff there is no automatic right of appeal against the decision as it is not a final interlocutor [3]. Finally it should be noted that parties to current or prospective civil proceedings may apply to the court for an order for the inspection, photographing, preservation, custody and detention of documents and other property if it appears to the court that a question relevantly arises as to that property in any civil proceedings extant or likely to be brought [4].

[1] SCR 37.

[2] A commissioner in this context is usually a named senior solicitor appointed by the court. If the documents are not provided, the other party can fix a commission which is a formal hearing before the commissioner where the party against whom the order was made either produces the documents or explains his/her reasons for not doing so.

[3] An interlocutor is the written ruling of the court on any procedural step in the case. See the Sheriff Courts (Scotland) Act 1907, section 37, and *City of Edinburgh District Council v Robbin* 1994 SCLR 43.

[4] Administration of Justice (Scotland) Act 1972, section 1.

14 LAW REFORM PROPOSALS

The law does not provide the answer to neighbour nuisance. Neither does law reform, although improvements can no doubt always be made. Many proposals for reform are an attempt to be seen to be 'doing something' about neighbour nuisance, but will amount to little more in practice than an attack on tenants' rights without materially affecting the perceived issues. Further research and understanding of the causes of neighbour nuisance are required before knee jerk 'solutions' are proposed.

14.1 In May 1995 the Scottish Office published a consultation paper on probationary secure tenancies [1]. This move mirrors similar proposals made earlier that year by the Department of Environment in respect of English and Welsh tenancies. The paper is in response to growing concern about anti-social behaviour. The proposal is that a secure tenancy is a 'valuable asset' and should be 'earned'. At present, tenants of local authorities, Scottish Homes and Development Corporations are secure tenants in terms of the Housing (Scotland) Act 1987. Secure tenants enjoy security of tenure; that is, a landlord may only evict on certain specified grounds and in most cases the court must be satisfied that it is reasonable to evict. In summary, the Scottish Office proposals were as follows. All public sector landlords would be given the discretionary power to introduce probationary tenancies. Where a landlord does so, they will apply to all new tenants; that is, groups or individuals could not be singled out for probationary tenancies. The probationary tenancy would last for the first 12 months of the tenancy. Providing the tenancy had not been terminated before the end of that 12 month period, it would automatically convert into a secure tenancy. It could be terminated at any time within the 12 month period by a notice to quit giving at least 28 days' notice. The consultation paper did not propose that the landlord's rights to terminate the tenancy be limited in any way. That is, the landlord could terminate the tenancy for any reason, not just alleged anti-social behaviour. Any tenant served with a notice to quit would have a right to a review of the decision. The review would be carried out by the landlord itself (a housing sub-committee is suggested) before the expiry of the notice to quit. If the tenant failed to remove, court action for ejection would be required. The landlord would have a right to such an order for ejection provided the notice to quit was valid. However, none of the usual requirements relating to actions for recovery of possession of secure tenancies would be required. In particular the landlord would not be required to prove the reasons for terminating the tenancy. Nor would the landlord have to show that it was reasonable to grant a decree for ejection. In England and Wales, the Housing Act 1996 has now brought into force a new type of tenancy: the introductory tenancy, which is essentially the same as the proposed probationary tenancy [2]. At the time of writing, the view of the Scottish Office is unknown.

[1] Scottish Office Environment Department (1995) *Anti-social Behaviour on Housing Estates: Consultation Paper on Probationary Tenancies*, Scottish Office.

[2] See 14.4 infra.

14.2 The proposals attracted considerable opposition from a range of sources including tenants groups, academics, lawyers, representatives of land-lords and even public sector landlords themselves [1]. The reasons for opposition were many. The principal reasons can be summarised as follows [2]:

- The proposals are unnecessary. Other options exist.
- Tenants would have no real protection against an eviction action on any ground, whether justified or not.
- The proposals are premature – little research has as yet been done.
- They would affect all new tenants even though those causing neighbour nuisance are a small minority.
- The proposals assume that anti-social behaviour is likely to reveal itself soon after the start of the tenancy. There is no evidence for this; the contrary may be true.
- Security of tenure is an important principle which should not be subject to local variation.
- There is no independent right to review. Any challenge to a decision would have to be by way of judicial review.
- The most needy, such as those entering community care, would be vulnerable to unfair complaints.
- Landlords already have powers to create temporary tenancies under both the assured and secure tenancy regimes
- Probationary tenancies would considerably increase the workload of housing departments.

[1] See, for example, submissions to Scottish Office by Professor Donnison et al. Glasgow University, the Scottish Association of Law Centres, the Chartered Institute of Housing, Scottish Federation of Housing Associations and Shelter Scotland, and COSLA.

[2] Acknowledgements to Donnison et al. (1995) and J. J. Mitchell, QC.

14.3   A variation on the proposals has been suggested by some, notably Dundee District Council. They suggest that landlords should have the right to elect to offer probationary tenancies in particular cases where the landlord has reason to suspect that the prospective tenant may offend or fail to pay rent. Many of the objections noted above would apply to such a proposal. More specific objections in relation to such a proposal have been made [1]:

- It is wrong to equate rent arrears with anti-social behaviour.
- It would be difficult to prove a prospective tenant had been guilty of anti social behaviour in the past. Determining this question would lead to a number of practical and technical difficulties negating its value.
- There is a danger that vulnerable persons or groups (e.g. community care returners) may be singled out for such tenancies.

[1]   Submission by Chartered Institute of Housing in Scotland to Scottish Office in response to consultation paper, 1995.

14.4   The Housing Act 1996, which applies only to England and Wales, contains numerous provisions in Part V apparently designed to improve the powers of landlords to deal with anti-social conduct in housing cases. The provisions can be summarised as follows.

- Introductory tenancies may be offered for a one-year period. This proposal is almost identical to probationary tenancies which are discussed above.
- Amendment to the grounds for recovery of possession of secure and assured tenancies so that it is sufficient that the nuisance is caused to a person 'residing, visiting or otherwise engaging in a lawful action in the vicinity of the house', thus widening its scope.
- Introduction of a new ground for eviction of secure and assured tenants where one partner has left the dwellinghouse as a result of the violence of the other and the house is thus under-occupied.
- Allowing eviction proceedings to commence on service of the notice of proceedings (rather than waiting for expiry of the 28-day notice period).
- The court will have the power to attach a power of arrest to an injunction obtained by a social landlord where that injunction is in respect of a breach of the tenancy agreement relating to various types of anti-social behaviour. The power to arrest may also be attached to ex-parte injunctions. The power to arrest may also be sought by a local authority seeking an injunction against anti-social behaviour using its powers under section 222 of the Local Government Act 1972. Where such a power of arrest is granted, the police may arrest any person restrained by the injunction where they have cause to suspect s/he may be in breach of

the injunction. Such a power is similar to that already available in respect of matrimonial interdicts [1].

[1] In Scotland, under the Matrimonial Homes (Family Protection)(Scotland) Act 1981.

14.4.1   In the authors' view, with the possible exception of the last provision, such proposals are not to the point. Objections to introductory/probationary tenancies are noted above. Extending the scope of the nuisance and annoyance ground is unlikely to make any real change in practice: the authors know of no reported Scottish cases which have turned on a narrow definition of the persons affected or vicinity. The introduction of the new ground does not deal with anti-social behaviour directly at all. Allowing eviction proceedings to commence immediately on service of the notice of proceedings is simply tokenistic: where the proceedings are defended, the extra 28 days gained are unlikely to be significant. Furthermore, it detracts from one of the purposes of the notice which is to give a warning that court proceedings may commence after 28 days if an improvement in behaviour is not made. It is contrary to the incremental approach advocated by the present writers [1]. Anti-social behaviour in housing is a complex phenomenon and solutions are much more likely to be found in non-legal management based remedies. The provisions in the Act taken as a whole are likely, at best, to be simply ineffective as the root causes of anti-social behaviour are entirely ignored.

[1] See Chapter 2 above.

14.5 Other proposals for legislative change have been made in Scotland [1]. First, there could be a statutory provision implying a term into all tenancy agreements with regard to nuisance. Such implied terms already exist: for example, in relation to repairs [2]. The exact wording of the term would be a matter for debate. The effect would be to allow the courts to consider such matters as a general matter applying across the country rather than as a matter of interpretation of each contract [3]. It would be of value from April 1996 now that the unitary authorities have, in many cases, inherited a number of forms of lease of variable quality. It would give court decisions a national value and make commentaries on the decisions and the law universal. Parliament would also be enabled to demonstrate its concern on the subject.

[1] Acknowledgements to Jonathan Mitchell, QC.

[2] Housing (Scotland) Act 1987, section 113 and Schedule 10.

[3] Where, of course, the landlord is founding on a breach of a tenancy condition forbidding certain behaviour.

14.5.1 Secondly, local authorities could be given express power to pursue proceedings for interdict. The effect of recent cases [1] has been to cast doubt on the right of a district council to such an interdict on behalf of one of its tenants against a non-tenant. English local authorities presently have such powers. In addition, the procedure for taking action following an alleged breach of interdict should be considerably simplified. Rather than raising a fresh action, the Pursuer should be able to proceed in the interdict action itself, perhaps by way of minute and answers.

[1] *Dundee District Council v Cook* 1995 SCLR (N) 559; *Edinburgh District Council, Petrs* 1990 SCLR 511.

14.5.2 In eviction actions, the range of powers of the courts to deal with the issue at hand should be made more explicit. Thus, the courts presently have the power in eviction cases to adjourn the case without passing judgment, subject to such conditions as the court sees fit [1]. For example, in *Dundee District Council v Rice* [2], the case was adjourned after proof subject to the condition that the tenant defender would not live with her cohabitee (who was the cause of the nuisance). In another recent case, decree was granted but suspended subject to the condition that the tenant seek help for her alcohol problem [3]. Although these powers presently exist, they appear to be seldom used. See also the various recommendations made in the Report of the Scottish Affairs Select Committee on this subject, published in December 1996 [4].

[1] 1987 Act, section 48; 1988 Act, section 20.

[2] (Unrep.) 8th October 1991, Dundee Sheriff Court, Sheriff Raeburn.

[3] *Govanhill Housing Association v MacKenzie* (unrep.) 7th July 1995, Glasgow Sheriff Court, Sheriff Peebles.

[4] Cmnd. 196.

APPENDIX

FURTHER READING

(A) **LEGAL TEXTS**

Bridges and Forbes (1990), *Making the Law work against Racial Harassment*, Legal Action Group.

Burn-Murdoch (1933), *Interdict.*

Cross and Tapper (1985), *Cross on Evidence.*

Dickson (1887), *A Treatise on the Law of Evidence in Scotland*, Greens.

Field, D. (1988), *The Law of Evidence in Scotland*, Greens.

Field, D. and Rait, F. (1997), *The Law of Evidence in Scotland*, Greens.

Field, D. (1989), *Civil Evidence (Scotland) Act 1988* (annotated), Greens.

Henderson and O'Carroll (1994), *Town and Country Planning in Scotland: Powers and Procedures*, Hillside Publishing.

Himsworth (1995), *Housing Law in Scotland,* Planning Exchange/ Butterworths.

Hughes (1992), *Environmental Law*, Butterworths.

MacPhail (1987), *Evidence (Revised Research Papers)*, Law Society of Scotland.

MacPhail, (1987), *Sheriff Court Practice*, Greens.

Mitchell, J. (1994), *Eviction and Rent Arrears*, Shelter (Scotland).

Mullen, T. (1987), *A Guide to Judicial Review in Scotland*, Shelter (Scotland).

Mullen (1990), 'Representation at Tribunals' in *Modern Law Review*, pp 64–92.

Mullen (ed.) (1992), *Scottish Housing Law Handbook,* Sweet & Maxwell.

Paton and Cameron (1967), *Landlord and Tenant*, Greens.

Pugh-Smith (1994), *Neighbours and the Law (1994)*, Sweet & Maxwell (English Law only).

Rankine (1916), *Law of Leases in Scotland*, Greens.

Reid (1996), *Housing and Anti-social Behaviour: Practice Note on the Use of Legal Remedies*, Chartered Institute of Housing in Scotland.

Robson, *Housing (Scotland) Act 1986,* (annotations and commentary), Greens.

Robson (1995), *Residential Tenancies*, Greens.

Scott-Robinson (1994), *The Law of Interdict* (contained in *Stair Memorial Encyclopaedia*), Butterworths.

Scottish Law Commission Report No. 118, *Recovery of Possession of Heritable Property*, HMSO.

Tromans, Nash and Poustie (1996), *Environmental Protection Act 1990* (annotated), Sweet & Maxwell.

Walker (1975), *Civil Remedies*, Greens.

Walker and Walker (1964), *The Law of Evidence*, Hodge.

Watchman, P. Q. (1990), 'The Rights of Secure Tenants', (1990) J.L.S.S 425.

Watchman, P. Q. (1991), '*Housing (Scotland) Act 1987* – (annotations and commentary), Greens, Sweet & Maxwell.

Wilkinson (1986), *The Scottish Law of Evidence*, Butterworths/Law Society of Scotland.

(B) NON–LEGAL TEXTS

Aldbourne Associates (1993), *Managing Neighbour Complaints in Social Housing: A Handbook for Practitioners*, Aldbourne Associates.

Association of District Councils (1994), *Winning Communities, the role of housing including promoting community safety*, London, ADC.

Bannister, J. and Kearns, A. (1995), *Managing Crime: Findings from a Survey of Scottish Housing Initiatives*, Edinburgh, Chartered Institute of Housing.

Belgrave, Susan (1995), *Nuisance and Harassment: Law and Practice in the Management of Social Housing*, London, Lemos.

Bright, J. (1993) 'Everybody Needs Good Neighbours' in *Inside Housing*, Feb. 1993.

Brown, L. (1992), *Neighbourhood Watch: A literature review*, Edinburgh, Central Research Unit, Scottish Office.

Burns, Danny and Williams, Malcolm (1989), *Neighbourhood Working: A New Manual*, Chartered Institute of Housing, Coventry.

Chartered Institute of Housing (1995), *Good Practice Briefing No. 3: Neighbour Nuisance: Ending the Nightmare*, CIoH.

Clapham, D., Kintrea, K., Malcolm J., Parkey, H. and Scott, S. (1995), *A Baseline Study of Housing Management in Scotland*, Edinburgh, Scottish Office Central Research Unit, HMSO.

Coleman, Alice (1985), *Utopia on Trial*, Hilary Shipman.

Conklin, J. (1975), *The Impact of Crime*, New York, MacMillan.

Damer, Sean (1989), *From Moorepark to Wine Alley*, Edinburgh University Press.

Department of Environment (1989), *Tackling Racial Violence and Harassment in Local Authority Housing*, HMSO.

Appendix

Department of Environment (1990), *Report of the Noise Review Working Party*, HMSO.

Department of Environment (1992), *Proposed Legislation Response to Recommendations in Noise Review Report*, DoE.

Department of Environment (1992b), *Control of Noisy Parties*, DoE and Home Office.

Department of Environment (1993), *Crime Prevention on Council Estates*, HMSO.

Department of Environment (1994), *Mediation: Benefits and Practice*, London, Department of Environment.

Department of Environment (1994b), *Racial Incidents in Council Housing: The Local Authority Response*, HMSO.

DoE, Department of Transport, Department of Education and Science, Scottish Office, Welsh Office (1991) *Environmental Protection Act 1990: Code of Practice on Litter and Refuse*, HMSO.

Department of Environment, Welsh Office and Scottish Office (1995), *Neighbour Noise Working Party: Review of the Effectiveness of Neighbour Noise Controls*, DoE, Welsh Office and Scottish Office.

Donnison, David (1995), *The Neat and Tidy v The Poor and Needy* in *Scotland on Sunday*, 2nd July 1995.

Eldridge, J., Madigan, R. and Daglian, S. (1982), *Neighbour Disputes: The Response of Glasgow's Housing Department to Tenants' Complaints*, Glasgow, Sociology Department, University of Glasgow.

Forbes, D. (1983), *Action on Racial Harassment*, Legal Action Group.

Foster, Janet and Hope, Tim (1993), *Housing, Community and Crime: The Impact of the Priority Estates Project*, Home Office Research Study No. 131, HMSO.

Glennerster, H., and Turner, T., (1993), *Estate Based Housing Management: An Evaluation*, DoE/HMSO.

Goldie, David (1992) 'Neighbour Complaints in Edinburgh', Dissertation submitted for the M.Phil in Housing Studies, University of Glasgow.

Hughes, D. (1992), *Environmental Law*, London, Butterworths.

Hughes, D. J., Karn, V. A. and Liskeleiss, R. (1994), 'Neighbour Disputes, Social Landlords and the Law' in Journal of Social Welfare and Family Law, pp 201–228.

Hunter, Lawrence (1994), *Occasional Paper on Housing No. 7, Wakening up the Neighbours – A Scottish Perspective on Neighbour Disputes*, Housing Policy and Practice Unit, University of Stirling.

IEHO (1992), *Environmental Health Statistics 1990/91*, Institution of Environmental Health Offices, London.

Jacobs, Jane (1961), *The Death and Life of Great American Cities*, New York, Vintage Books.

Appendix

Karn, Valerie, Lickiss, Rachel, Hughes, David and Crawley, John (1993), *Neighbour Disputes: Responses by Social Landlords*, Institute of Housing, Coventry.

Kearns, A. and Malcolm, J. (1994), *Housing Management Amongst Housing Associations in Scotland*, Edinburgh Scottish Homes.

Kelly, Patrick (1995), 'Anti-social antidotes' in *Roof, Vol. 20 No. 4 July/August 1995, pp 38–39.*

Keenan, B. (1992), 'Calming the Neighbours' in *Housing,* June 1992, pp 50–51.

Keightley (1991), *Good Neighbours, Bad Neighbours*, Priority Estates Project (available from Lemos).

London Housing Consortium (1992), *Controlled Entry Systems in Local Authority Blocks of Flats – A handbook of good practice*, London Housing Consortium.

Mackay, R. and Moody, S. (1993), 'The environmental context of neighbour disputes' in Jones (ed.), *Crime and the Urban Environment*, Avebury.

Mackay, R. and Moody, S. and Walker (1994), *Neighbour Disputes in the Criminal Justice System*, Scottish Office Central Research Unit, Edinburgh.

Maynard, Warwick (1994), *Witness Intimidation; Strategies for Prevention*, Home Office Police Department, London.

Mediation UK (1993), *Guide to Starting a Community Mediation Service*, Mediation UK.

Mediation UK (1994), *Directory of Mediation and Conflict Resolution Services*, Mediation UK.

Michel, Paul (1995), *The Noisy Neighbour Survival Guide*, Spot on Publishing, Wigan.

Morton, Tim (1991), *Dogs on the Lead: Good Practice for Dogs on Housing Estates*, Priority Estates Project.

Mullen, T. and Scott, S. (1995), *If probationary tenancies are the answer – What was the question? Occasional Paper 22*, Glasgow: Centre for Housing Research and Urban Studies, University of Glasgow.

Murray, Charles (1990), *The Emerging British Underclass*, London, Institute of Economic Affairs.

National Association for the Care and Resettlement of Offenders (1988), *Growing up on Housing Estates: A Review of the Play and Recreational Needs of Young People*, London, NACRO.

National Consumer Council (1991), *Housing Complaints Procedures: Principles of Good Practice for Social Landlords*, NCC.

National Housing and Town Planning Council (1992), *High Rise Housing* (2nd ed.), NHTPC.

Osborn and Shattoe (1995), *Safe Neighbourhoods? Success and Failure in Crime Prevention*, Safe Neighbourhood Unit.

Osborn, S. and Bright, J. (1989), *Crime Prevention and Community Safety – A Practical Guide for Local Authorities*, NACRO.

Page, David (1993), *Building for Communities: A Study of New Housing Association Estates*, Joseph Rowntree Foundation.

Page, David (1994), *Developing Communities*, Sutton Hastoe HA.

Popplestone, G. (1981), 'Difficult tenants: who they are and what to do about them' in *CES Review*.

Power, Ann (1987), *Property before People*, Allen and Unwin.

Power, Ann (1987), *The PEP Guide to Local Housing Management: Volume 1, The PEP Model*, Priority Estates Project/HMSO.

Power, Ann (1987), *The PEP Guide to Local Housing Management: Volume 2, The PEP Experience*, Priority Estates Project/HMSO.

Power, Ann (1987), *The PEP Guide to Local Housing Management: Volume 3, Guidelines for Setting up New Projects*, Priority Estates Project/HMSO/DoE.

Power, Ann (1991), *Housing Management: A Guide to Quality and Creativity*, Longman.

Poyner, B. (1982), *Design against Crime – beyond defensible space*, Butterworths.

Priority Estates Project (1992), *Clean Away: Keeping Housing Estates Clean*, Priority Estates Project.

Reid, Marian (1995), *Housing and Crime: How well are we managing: Practice note on housing management initiatives for tackling crime*, Chartered Institute of Housing in Scotland.

Safe Neighbourhoods Unit (1994), *Crime Prevention and Council Estates*, DoE/HMSO.

Safe Neighbourhood Unit (1994), *High Expectations: A guide to the development of concierge schemes and controlled access in high rise social housing*, HMSO.

Safe Neighbourhood Unit (1994), *Managing to make neighbourhoods safer*, Safe Neighbourhood Unit.

Sainsbury, R. and Eardley, T. (1991), *Housing Benefit Reviews*, London, Department of Social Security Research Report Series No. 3.

Saunders, Roger (1993), *The New Housing Manager: Generic Working in Local Housing Offices*, Priority Estates Project.

Scott, C. (1995), 'Landlord Interdicts: the experience of Edinburgh District Council', Housing Diploma Research Paper, University of Stirling.

Scott, Suzie (ed.) (1991), *Neighbour Disputes – Is there an answer?*, Glasgow, TPAS (Scotland).

Scott, Suzie (ed.) (1994), *Housing and Anti-social Behaviour – The Way Ahead*, Chartered Institute of Housing in Scotland.

Scott, Suzie (1994), *Reviewing Good Practice* (IoH Scotland conference paper), Glasgow University Centre for Housing Research and Urban Studies.

Scottish Office Environment Department (1994a), *Housing and Crime Prevention*, Env. Circular 2/1994, Scottish Office.

Scottish Office Environment Department (1995), *Anti-social Behaviour on Housing Estates: Consultation Paper on Probationary Tenancies*, Scottish Office.

Seager and Jeffries (1994), *Elementary Racial Harassment: A guide to housing policies and procedures*, London, Lemos.

Tebay, Cumberbatch and Graham (1986), *Disputes Between Neighbours*, Aston University.

Tenant Participation Advisory Service (1995), *Neighbour Disputes and Anti social Behaviour, a Discussion Paper,* TPAS.

University of Stirling in conjunction with the Chartered Institute of Housing in Scotland (1995), *Good Practice in Housing Management: Guidance Note No. 5, Tenancy Management*, Scottish Office.

Wilson Committee on the Problem of Noise (1963), *Noise: Final Report*, Cmnd 2056, HMSO.

Zipfel, Tricia (1994), *On Target: Extending Partnership to Tackle Problems on Estates*, Priority Estates Project.

USEFUL ADDRESSES

Aldbourne Associates, Ulmus, Ogbourne Road, Aldbourne, Wiltshire SN8 2LD. Tel. 01672-515005.

Butterworths, 4 Hill Street, Edinburgh EH2 3JZ. Tel. 0131-224 7828.

Chartered Institute of Housing in Scotland, 6 Palmerston Place, Edinburgh. Tel. 0131-225 4544.

Chartered Institute of Housing, Good Practice Unit, Octavia House, Westwood Way, Coventry CV4 8JP. Tel. 01203-474814.

Commission for Racial Equality, 100 Princes Street, Edinburgh. Tel: 0131 226 5186.

Commissioner for Local Administration in Scotland (The Ombudsman), Princes House, 5 Shandwick Place, Edinburgh. Tel. 0131-225 5300.

Greens, 21 Alva Street, Edinburgh EH2 4PS. Tel. 0131-225 4879.

Hillside Publishing, 9 Woodside Cottages, Sheilhill Road, Tealing, Dundee DD4 0PW.

Law Society of Scotland, 26 Drumsheugh Gardens, Edinburgh EH3 7YR. Tel. 0131-226 7411.

Legal Services Agency Ltd, 11th Floor, Fleming House, 134 Renfrew Street, Glasgow G3 6ST. Tel. 0141-353 3354.

Mediation UK, 82a Gloucester Road, Bristol BS7 8BN. Tel. 0117-924 1234.

Scottish Association of Law Centres, 6 Harmony Row, Glasgow G51 3BA. Tel. 0141-445 6451, Fax 0141-440 5423.

Scottish Federation of Housing Associations, 6 York Place, Edinburgh. Tel. 0131-556 5777.

Tenant Participation Advisory Service, 22 St. Andrew Street, Glasgow. Tel: 0141-552 3633.

GLOSSARY

Words in **bold** are glossed elsewhere in this glossary.

Action	(As in raising a legal action): a court case.
Affidavit	See paragraph 13.4.3.2.
Answers	The formal legal written document being the response to a **summary application** lodged by the **respondent**. Also used in **ordinary cause actions** to denote the response of the **defender** to each **averment** made by the **pursuer.**
Applicant	Person pursuing legal action under **summary application** procedure.
Averment	(Also, to aver) any statement or allegation of fact made in written legal **pleadings**.
Burden of proof	See paragraph 13.2.
Common law	The law other than law made by Parliament.
Corroboration	See paragraph 13.5.2.
Court of Session	The highest civil court in Scotland. It includes the Outer House (where civil **actions** are begun if not begun in the sheriff court) and the Inner House (which deals mainly with appeals from the Outer House and the sheriff court). Its decisions bind all other courts in Scotland. Appeal from the Inner House, where competent, is to the House of Lords.
Crave	Formal request contained in written legal pleadings to the court for a particular remedy (for example **decree** for **recovery of possession** or payment).

Decree	Court order. Decree may be in terms of the pursuer's **crave(s)**, or of dismissal (of the action) or absolvitor (a finding that the pursuer is not entitled to that which is craved and that the defender is immune from further action). Also decree ad factum praestandum, or specific implement (an order obliging the defender to carry out a specified act).
Defences	The formal legal written document being the response to a **summons** or **initial writ lodged** by a **defender**.
Defender	Person or body against whom legal action is pursued (the **respondent** if **summary application** procedure is used). There may be more than one defender.
Domicile	Loosely, the usual residence of a person or body.
Expenses	The usual rule is that the legal expenses of the successful litigant are paid by the losing side. Where the losing side is legally aided the court will usually reduce the expenses, often to nil.
Et seq.	And that which follows.
Ex parte	In the absence of a party to the action. Also used in the citation of some types of English cases where the name following ex parte would in Scotland be termed the **pursuer**. Often abbreviated to ex p.
Hearsay	See paragraphs 13.4.1 *et seq*.
Inter alia	Among other things (plural: inter alios).
Inner House (IH)	See **Court of Session.**
Induciae	A time limit. Usually found in the context of **service** of a **summons** or **initial writ**.
Infra	Below.

Initial writ	The formal legal document lodged and served by a **pursuer** to commence (e.g.) an **ordinary cause action**.
Interdict	(And interim interdict). See Chapter 4.
Irritancy clause	A provision in a lease allowing (usually) the landlord to terminate the lease if a specified event occurs (for example non-payment of rent).
Ish	Date on which a lease ends: the last day of the term of the lease.
Lodge (to)	To formally deposit a court document in the court **process.**
Notice of Proceedings	See paragraph 7.3.1.
Notice to Quit	See paragraph 7.2.2.
Ordinary Cause	A type of sheriff court procedure more formal than both **summary cause procedure** and **summary application**. Used, for example, in interdict actions.
Outer House (OH)	See **Court of Session.**
Pleadings	Collectively, the **summons**, or **initial writ**, or **summary applications**, the **defences/answers** together with any other formal written statement of a party's position **lodged** in court.
Precognition	See paragraph 13.4.3.2.
Prima facie	At first sight.
Procurator fiscal	Lawyer employed by the state who prosecutes those accused of criminal charges in the sheriff court.
Process	The collection of legal documents lodged in court which relate to a particular court **action.**

Productions	Those documents, containing evidence, **lodged** in court, on which a party intends to rely to pursue or defend his/her case.
Proof	Contested civil court hearing where evidence is led by all parties (equivalent to a trial under criminal procedure).
Pursuer	The person or body initiating legal action (the **applicant** if summary application procedure used). There may be more than one pursuer.
Recovery of possession of heritable property	Eviction **action**.
Respondent	Person or body against whom **summary application** is being sought. Or, person or body defending an appeal.
Service	Formal legal delivery of a document.
Sheriff	Name for the judge who decides cases in the **sheriff court**. Appeal, where competent, is usually to the **sheriff principal** for that **sheriffdom**. His/her decisions are not binding on any other sheriff.
Sheriff Court	Local court used for initiating most housing **actions** such as eviction or **interdict**. Civil cases are heard by a single **sheriff**.
Sheriffdom	Scotland is divided into six sheriffdoms. Each sheriffdom has one **sheriff principal**, at least one **sheriff court** and a number of **sheriffs**.
Sheriff officers	Court officials employed by private firms who carry out various duties associated with legal proceedings (such as **serving summonses**).

Glossary

Sheriff Principal   Each **sheriffdom** has one sheriff principal who hears appeals from the decisions of the **sheriffs** and who has various administrative functions in connection with the administration of the **sheriffdom**. His decisions are binding on all **sheriffs** within that **sheriffdom**. Appeal is to the **Inner House** of the **Court of Session.**

Sist (to/a)   A court order suspending progress of the court case, usually to allow some other action to take place (for example, to make an application for legal aid, or to allow negotiations). A court case may be sisted at any time by the court.

Specific implement *(Or ad factum praestandum)* See **decree.**

Standard of proof   See paragraph 13.3.1.

Statute   Act of Parliament.

Summary Application Procedure   Least formal court procedure. Used in a range of legal **actions**, for example, complaints under Section 82 of the Environmental Protection Act 1990. The action is commenced by **service** of a document known as a summary application.

Summary Cause   A type of sheriff court procedure less formal than **ordinary cause.** Used for most eviction actions and for payment **actions** between £750 and £1500. The **action** is commenced by **service** of a **summons**.

Summons   The formal legal document used to commence a **summary cause action** or small claims action.

Supra   Above.

Tacit relocation   Legal concept whereby a lease for a fixed period is automatically renewed for a similar period on the same terms in the absence of effective termination at the **ish** by either party.

INDEX